WISDOM FOR THE JOURNEY

Wisdom for the Journey

*Conversations with Spiritual Fathers
of the Christian East*

SERGE BOLSHAKOFF

Epilogue by
M. Basil Pennington, OCSO

ALBA·HOUSE   **alba house**   NEW·YORK

SOCIETY OF ST. PAUL, 2187 VICTORY BLVD., STATEN ISLAND, NEW YORK 10314

ST PAULS

Library of Congress Cataloging-in-Publication Data

Bolshakoff, Serge.
  Wisdom for the journey: conversations with spiritual fathers of the
Christian East / Serge Bolshakoff; epilogue by M. Basil Pennington.
      p.   cm.
  Includes bibliographical references.
  ISBN 0-8189-0836-X
  1. Monastic and religious life. 2. Spirituality — Orthodox Eastern
Church. 3. Bolshakoff, Serge. I. Title.
  BX581.B65 2000
  248.4'819 — dc21   99-059478

Produced and designed in the United States of America by the
Fathers and Brothers of the Society of St. Paul,
2187 Victory Boulevard, Staten Island, New York 10314-6603,
as part of their communications apostolate.

ISBN: 0-8189-0836-X

Printing Information:

Current Printing - first digit   1   2   3   4   5   6   7   8   9   10

Year of Current Printing - first year shown

2001   2002   2003   2004   2005   2006   2007   2008   2009   2010

Table of Contents

PART IV: MOUNT ATHOS

PART V: FRANCE

Introduction

This book is a selection of the writings of Dr. Serge Bolshakoff. It begins with a few accounts of conversations during his childhood in Russia at the beginning of this century but it is largely made up of those he had with monastic fathers of the Russian Orthodox Church. These took place between 1919 and 1974 in Russia, Estonia, Finland, on Mount Athos and in France. Until now they have been scattered among various books and manuscripts.

They have a vivid quality so that we can feel ourselves, sometimes after an account of a long journey to a remote monastery, being drawn alongside the author into the presences of these great teachers of life and religion as they talk with him. They are profoundly enlightening about Eastern Orthodox spirituality. These qualities derive from the nature of the encounters; they are between a man of devout Orthodox faith with an unusual skill for interviewing and then recording what was said and men advanced in the life of prayer, some of whom were true mystics.

We have two aims in publishing these writings: to bring amidst us again our friend Serge Bolshakoff and to pass on his message and experience.

In his preface to the second volume of the Doctor's *Recollections*, Father Basil Pennington wrote: "Doctor Bolshakoff was a unique man, with a unique vocation. Only heaven knows the full extent of the contribution he has made to bring Christians, sadly divided, back together again." Doctor Bolshakoff's vocation was, in part, to make Eastern Orthodox spirituality better known to people of Western countries. Equally important to him was the promotion of Christian unity. In this he was in the tradition of his compatriot, the famous philosopher, Vladimir Soloviev (1853-1900). The practice of the Prayer of the Heart and his thoughts on this prayer form an integral part of his message. The encounters he had with monastic fathers, building on conversations he had as a child, clearly made a deep impression on him and were experiences central to his life's work.

Even a brief account of the author's life will tell us much of how he lived out his vocation. He was born in St. Petersburg in 1901 into a wealthy, cultured and religious family. After his secondary education he began to study civil engineering. In 1919, to escape the consequences of the Communist Revolution, Bolshakoff left Russia for Estonia. He returned to Russia once later in life for a short visit but he never lived there again. In Estonia he continued his former studies, then he turned to economics and sociology and finally to theology. In the course of the next few decades he traveled widely in Europe in the cause of ecumenism and of social justice based on Christian ethics. He often visited monasteries, mostly Benedictine and Cistercian. During the course of the Second World War and for a few years afterwards he resided at Oxford and studied at Christ Church where in 1943 he completed a doctorate in philosophy. In 1951 his fiancée died in a car accident and after this tragic event he traveled more frequently. In fact, moving from monastery to monastery, staying for a few weeks or a few months, became his way of life. Aided by his linguistic skills, he was able to contact many men of religion, some highly placed. At the monasteries he wrote and he prayed.

In 1974, after many years of travel, Doctor Bolshakoff finally settled at Hauterive Abbey, in Switzerland. There he remained, continuing to write his books and keeping up a large personal correspondence until his death in 1990 at the age of eighty-nine.

Serge Bolshakoff remained a layman and described himself as a writer on religious subjects. The list of his publications, which are in several languages, is a long one. It is made up of works, always scholarly, on the historical and social aspects of Christianity, ecumenism, prayer and mysticism. Some have a personal quality, like the conversations published here.

These conversations remind us of those reported by the author of that classic, *The Way of a Pilgrim*.[1] Between the two authors there are differences but their lives, as well as their writings, had much in common. They spent a great part of their time traveling and had no permanent home. They practiced constant prayer and placed their trust in Divine Providence.

Serge Bolshakoff has been underestimated in the past, although not by everyone who knew him and his works. Thomas Merton, the well-known Cistercian writer, in his Preface to Dr. Bolshakoff's *Russian Mystics*,[2] welcomed this learned work and wrote that it had too modest a title. But one does not have to seek far to find the reason for Bolshakoff's being undervalued. Norris Merchant, a professor of philosophy and comparative religion in the USA, in reviewing *Russian Mystics*,[3] spoke of the author's lack in it of criticism of the teaching of these mystics and perceptively pointed out that this was in keeping with the advice of the Staretz Ambrose. Ambrose was the model for Dostoevsky's Father Zosima in the novel, *The Brothers Karamazov*. Ambrose advised all to "live without sadness, judge no one, trouble no one, and to revere everyone." Serge Bolshakoff, in spite of his wide erudition, tended to avoid philosophical and religious debate and any form of confrontation. He lived the advice of Ambrose. This is confirmed by those who knew him.

In some ways the teaching in these conversations is more appropriate for the monk rather than the laymen but the teachers are not closed to the belief that true holiness can be found in the lay life. This is illustrated by the account of a young man, Sergei Mironovitch Paul. Paul was an accomplished, highly educated and devout layman who entered a monastery and very much wanted to stay there. But his spiritual father sent him out into the world, judging this to be a better place for him to become truly holy. (See Chapter 10)

The question may be asked: Are we reading the actual words spoken by these fathers or are we receiving the author's interpreta-

---

[1] Doubleday, NY, 1978 and New Sarov Press, Blanco, Texas, USA, 1993.

[2] Cistercian Studies Series, No. 26 (Kalamazoo, MI: Cistercian Publications), 1976 and 1981.

[3] *Parabola*, III, 2, 1979, pp. 114-115.

tion or elaboration of what the fathers said? Dr. Bolshakoff had an unusually retentive memory and he had a deep respect for factual reality even in matters of detail. So the events that he describes are likely to be exactly what took place and his accounts of conversations are probably very close to what was actually said.

These writings have an autobiographical dimension. The fathers respond to the individual and his personal situation. This can be clearly seen in the encounters with Father Ilian and even more so in those with Father Michael. The latter seemed to know intuitively the author's needs and he made these the starting point for his teaching. In an early chapter the author reveals that he is searching for his way in life, reflecting that through these encounters he "may yet find his true vocation and the way to realize it."

There is a poetry in these writings. It breaks through in the descriptions of landscapes and monasteries. Thus transformed they symbolize the deeper meaning of the text. The journey that Bolshakoff paints is an icon of the spiritual journey. In the course of these travels this searching man of God found much deep Christian meaning and in these accounts he seeks to share it with us. It has been the joy of four of us to collaborate with our friend Serge in this endeavor as we prepared these writings for publication.

On September 21, 1990, Dr. Serge Bolshakoff died in Switzerland at the Monastery of Hauterive. His funeral on the twenty-fourth was a beautiful ecumenical ceremony. First there was a solemn Requiem Mass celebrated by the Cistercian Community of Hauterive, then a Russian Orthodox service conducted by a Russian Orthodox priest by the open coffin. After a small bag of Russian earth had been placed in the coffin, Serge Bolshakoff was buried in the cemetery of the Monastery of Hauterive.

COMPILERS: Hans Smith
Victor Gareau
Dr. Anthony Spalding
Miroslaw Ryzyk

The Hague, Holland

A Short Autobiography

Serge Bolshakoff was born in St. Petersburg, Russia, in 1901. His was a well-to-do and cultured family. For his secondary education he was sent to one of the best schools in the capital of the Empire. He was meant to become a civil engineer and he started with these studies. But very soon economics and sociology attracted him and then religious questions, ecumenism and mysticism. In 1925 the Conference on Life and Work in Stockholm presented new possibilities to him, and the foundation of the ecumenical monastery at Amay (now Chevetogne) in Belgium in the next year excited him. In 1927 he met Father Paul Couturier, promoter of the Week of Prayer for Christian Unity, and he worked with him to promote the observance of this week throughout the Churches. At the same time he was interested in the efforts being made by the "Christendom" group in England to promote social justice on the basis of Christian ethics. During these years he wrote for the *Social Justice Review* published in St. Louis, Missouri, and *La Chronique Sociale de France* of Lyon. Just before the Second World War he published a long series of articles in Russian on Anglican religious communities. These articles were meant to be published as a book but the war intervened.

In 1943 he received his doctorate in philosophy at Oxford. He was written in at Christ Church, the college that has given Great Britain thirteen Prime Ministers, eleven Viceroys of India, the philosopher John Locke, Lewis Carroll who wrote *Alice in Wonderland* and others.

In the years following he published in London: *The Christian Church and the Soviet State* (1942), *The Foreign Missions of the Russian Orthodox Church* (1943) and *The Doctrine of the Unity of the Church in the Works of Khomyakov and Moehler* (1946). The preface of this last book was written by Dr. William Temple, then Archbishop of Canterbury and President of the World Council of Churches, and an introduction by Metropolitan Germanos of Thyateira, Exarch for Western Europe of the Ecumenical Patriarch. At the same time he continued to publish in the United States: *Russian Nonconformity* (Philadelphia, 1950) and *Father Michael, Recluse of Uusi Valamo* (New York, 1959).

In 1962 Serge Bolshakoff published *I Mistici Russi* in Turin, Italy. For it Cardinal Tisserant, at that time Dean of the Sacred College, wrote a preface. He personally presented this work to Pope John XXIII, who took the opportunity to discuss with Bolshakoff some of the problems concerning the opening of the Second Vatican Council. The English version of this book was published in the United States in 1977 by Cistercian Publications. This edition has a preface written by Thomas Merton.

After the Second World War Serge Bolshakoff traveled extensively and wrote a long series of articles on post-war Europe which were published in St. Louis in the *Social Justice Review*. In 1971 he published his first book on the Jesus Prayer. It was written in Russian and published in Brussels. Soon after it appeared in German in Vienna.

Dr. Bolshakoff continued writing after settling in at the Abbey of Hauterive in Switzerland in 1974. During these last years he wrote mainly on mysticism and the Jesus Prayer. The experience of a long life spent in many countries and in different surroundings taught him that the problems of Christian unity and social justice are spiritual problems. They cannot be solved by conferences, congresses and controversies but only by living a Christian life, by prayer and by a willingness to sacrifice.

Hauterive, 1981

WISDOM FOR THE JOURNEY

Part I

Russia

In 1919 Serge Bolshakoff had to flee his native country because of the Bolshevik Revolution and the Civil War. More than fifty years later some of his memoirs concerning his youth were published and this part is made up of five of these. They shed light on his early years and the Russian Orthodox family life in which he grew up.

CHAPTER 1

Father Sergius

I met Father Sergius at the Lavra of Saint Alexander Nevsky when I was a schoolboy in St. Petersburg. Father Sergius was my confessor and I visited him periodically. He had an apartment of several rooms but he always received me in his study with its two large windows and parquet floor. In one corner there was a bookstand with a cross and an epitrachelion which he put on to hear confessions.

Many memories come to my mind when I think of the Lavra. I visited it often, beginning in 1908. Many of my relatives and friends of my family are buried in the cemetery of the Lavra, a true necropolis of the Empire. The Lavra was founded by Peter the Great in 1713 to be a model for other monasteries as well as a nursery of bishops. In the Orthodox Church, since the time of the early ecumenical councils, bishops are always monks. Compared to other great Russian monasteries the Lavra was unique in many respects. Usually Russian monasteries had many unordained monks and relatively few priests who served as confessors and celebrants at the Liturgy. In the Lavra there were in 1746 twenty-three priests and three deacons, with only four lay monks and four novices. The priest-monks, or hieromonks as they were called, were continually raised to the episcopate or sent as abbots to monasteries all over the Empire. Many of the monks of this lavra were originally professed in other monasteries and transferred to the Lavra in order to be prepared for high office. Two monks of the Lavra, Innocent Kulchitsky and Sophroney Nazarensky, were consecrated bishops of Irkutsk, in Siberia and later canonized. Another monk of the Lavra, Father Theodore Ushakoff, became Superior of the famous Desert of Sanaskar. Father Alexis Shestakov, a recluse, was the spiritual director of Czar Alexander I. In time the office of the Superior of the Lavra was united with that of the Metropolitan of St. Petersburg, who is the Primate of Russia.

At the time the Empire came to an end, the Lavra was an immense complex of magnificent baroque buildings with vast gardens. Besides the monastic community, it housed the Imperial Ecclesiastical Academy (the Faculty of Theology), the Seminary, the Palace of the Primate and other institutions. The community was made up of cultured and wealthy men who lived on the estate rather in the fashion found in the great monasteries of the French *ancien regime* on the eve of the revolution.

I often spoke with Father Sergius on prayer and the monastic life. "You, Serezha, are interested in the monks of Valaam and you are right," the hieromonk once said to me. "Their life is truly ascetic. They live on the island and are completely cut off from the vanities of the world and its temptations. Silence and a harsh northern environment surround them. They are true cenobites. They also have hermits and recluses. Their startzy teach them how to practice the Prayer of the Heart. Our life here is quite different. We live in the imperial capital, always with people, always with temptations. The Primate lives with us. The members of the Holy Synod often visit us. Archimandrites who are to be promoted to the episcopate spend their time of probation with us. Members of the imperial family, court dignitaries, government officials, diplomats, wealthy people come to us.

"Look around you and see how we live here. It is like being in a palace: self-contained apartments, parquet floors, servants. Our refectory is like a palatial banquet hall. Our food, although meatless, is very good. To the monks of Valaam all this is scandalous. They call us monks only by courtesy. And yet, Serezha, this isn't quite true. I

4

agree, of course, that monks should live apart from the world, fasting and praying in solitude, and not in the capital city and in comfort. Still the heart of the problem is not in these things but in the soul, in the interior castle. Of what use is it to live in the desert, as an early monastic father said, if our hearts are full of memories of past humiliations or if we despise others? It is quite possible to live in our Lavra, among people, and still attain to true holiness.

"There was a man who lived in Constantinople in the days of the Byzantine Empire who did just that and became a true saint. His name was Symeon. He was a wealthy aristocrat and lived in the capital all his life. Yet, thanks to prayer and a good life, he attained to great visions and transcendent wisdom and left remarkable writings. He is called the 'New Theologian.' The Church gives the title of 'Theologian' to only three saints: Saint John the Evangelist, Saint Gregory of Nazianzus and this Symeon. People can attain salvation everywhere and in any state of life. We also have our ascetics, but we do not publicize them. This is better."

"And who are they?" I asked.

"Father Theodore Ushakoff, for instance, Superior of the Desert of Sanaskar, in the diocese of Tambov. And the Hieroschimonk Alexis Shestakov, who lived during the reign of Alexander I. Have you heard of them, Serezha?"

Father went on to tell their story: "John Ushakoff came from an ancient and noble family that gave several noted men to Russia. He was born in the province of Yaroslav, on the upper Volga. In due course he joined the Imperial Guard and served in St. Petersburg. Once, when he and his friends had dined too well, one of them suddenly dropped dead. This incident impressed the young man of twenty very forcefully. He realized the vanity and uncertainty of a worldly life and the fact that all must die. He understood the words, 'In whatever state I find you, I will judge you.' Taking off his splendid uniform, John dressed himself as a beggar and left the capital without notifying anyone. He retired to the virgin forest of northern Dvina to take up the life of a hermit.

5

"Because Ushakoff had left his regiment without permission, he was considered a deserter, albeit an officer. Ushakoff could not remain for long in the Dvina forests, for they were full of deserters who were constantly pursued by the military police. He therefore moved southward, to Ploshansk Monastery. The abbot there could not receive him, because he was considered a deserter, but he gave him a hut in the neighboring forest for a hermitage. In 1745 Ushakoff was arrested as a deserter and sent to St. Petersburg to be punished. His case was reported to Empress Elizabeth, the pious daughter of Peter the Great. She pardoned Ushakoff and allowed him to become a professed monk in the Lavra in 1747. She herself was present at his profession.

"Because Father Theodore, as John Ushakoff was called after his profession, was a spiritual director of rare quality, crowds started coming to him for advice and instruction. Some monks became jealous and began telling other monks of the Lavra that Father Theodore was seeking cheap popularity, unbecoming in a monk. Faced with such fraternal jealousy, Father was allowed, in 1750, to retire to the celebrated monastery of Sarov, where Saint Seraphim was then living.

"In 1762 Father Theodore was ordained a priest and appointed Superior of Sanaskar Monastery. He did much for his monastery, but, unable to tolerate injustice, he severely criticized the local governor. Because of his criticism, the governor accused Father Theodore of fomenting a peasant rebellion. As a result, Father was confined for nine years in an ecclesiastical prison in the remote arctic Solovky Monastery on an island in the White Sea. When he was allowed to return to Sanaskar, Father Theodore again began to attract crowds of people, who came to him for instruction and counseling. At one period he also traveled to the Alexecusky Nunnery to confess and direct the Sisters but this was later forbidden him, again through envy. Father Theodore died in 1791. He might well be canonized as was Saint Seraphim.

"Remember, Serezha," added the holy monk, "no one wishing to follow our Lord can escape sorrows and persecutions. Father Theodore could not escape such testing. He was persecuted through envy and because of his truthfulness. People dislike being reprimanded."

Father Sergius then spoke of another example, the hieromonk and recluse Alexis, known in the world as Alexander Shestakov.

"Father Alexis also lived at the Saint Alexander Nevsky Lavra, but some time after Father Theodore. He was originally a serf and received his freedom only when he was sixty years old, in 1814. He first entered Savin-Storsjhevsky Monastery and then went to the Lavra of Saint Sergius of Radonezh, near Moscow. There he was speedily professed and ordained a priest on account of his remarkable spiritual qualities. Very soon he became confessor and spiritual director to Seraphim Glagolev, Metropolitan of Moscow and Abbot of the Lavra. When Metropolitan Seraphim was appointed to the Russian primacy in St. Petersburg, he took his confessor with him. In 1823, Shestakov became megaloschemos with the name of Alexis.

"In 1825, Emperor Alexander I came to the Lavra by night to consult Father Alexis before leaving for Taganrog, where he died. In spite of the fact that it was night, the Lavra community, headed by the Primate, met the Emperor at the gate with the bells ringing. A service of intercession was sung in the Katholicon. The Emperor venerated the relics of his ancestor, Saint Alexander Nevsky, Grand Duke of Vladimir. Afterward he went to see Father Alexis, accompanied by the Primate. The recluse had a peculiar cell. Its walls were covered with a black cloth halfway up. Before the wall stood a large crucifix with Our Lady and Saint John the Evangelist on either side. An oil lamp burned before the crucifix. Along another wall stood a long black bench. In the next room there was a black coffin covered with a black cloth. Nothing more.

"The saying is true, Serezha," continued the monk, "'Remember your last end and you will never sin.' In youth this truth is forgotten, but old men know it well. When a man's conscience is pure he is joyful. If you have sinned you must repent on the spot. The difference between ordinary people and hardened criminals is simple. The first repent after they have sinned and try to amend their lives, while the second do not. Thus they become accustomed to sin and gradually lose the capacity to repent. Indeed a godly life appears to them unnatural and foolish. Did you ever visit the imperial graves in the fortress of Saint Peter and Saint Paul?"

"Yes, I did. My godfather, my maternal uncle, served in the Imperial Guard and was attached to the fortress for a while. I visited him occasionally with my father. I also visited the fortress with my *dyadka*, Basil Suvorov, now a commissioned officer in the Grenadier Guard Regiment."

"Well, what did you see?"

"I was always astonished that so many people ordered the Panikhida before the tomb of the Emperor Paul and so many pilgrims gathered around it. All the other tombs were visited only by tourists and the curious."

"You see, Serezha, God's ways are not ours. The voice of the people is the voice of the Lord." He went on: "How are the saints canonized? A saintly man dies. People begin to celebrate Panikhida on his grave. They ask his intercession in various cases. For instance, people coming to the tomb of the Emperor Paul are either married couples in difficulties or those who have complicated court cases. Then people start to be healed through the intercession of the holy man. The coffin is opened and the relics exposed. When this happens the canonization is near. This happened with the canonization of Saint Tikhon of Zadonsk, Saint Innocent of Irkutsk and Saint Seraphim of Sarov. People in St. Petersburg venerate also the grave of the Blessed Xenia, a Fool for Christ's sake, who died nearly one hundred and fifty years ago and was buried in the Smolensky churchyard. Did you go there?"

"No," I replied.

"Go," he said sharply. "You will find much to meditate upon."

"Was the Emperor Paul a saint?" I asked, rather astonished.

"God only knows that," he answered, "but if the people venerate his memory and ask his intercession, he most likely was. You saw this yourself. There is no veneration of any other emperor, even Alexander II, who abolished serfdom. The high circles tried many times to stop the public veneration of Paul I as a scandal, and failed. The life of that emperor was hard and sorrowful. He suffered much during his life and was finally murdered. No one can be saved living comfortably. Paul I died because he cared for the weak and the oppressed and was hated by the strong and powerful. His son, Alexander I, all his life considered himself guilty of the death of his father, though perhaps he could not have prevented it. This guilty feeling troubled his conscience. Alexander I was handsome, charming, intelligent. He was successful in everything, yet he was always unhappy. He could not find peace of soul anywhere. After a long struggle he defeated Napoleon and entered Paris. He liberated many European countries conquered by Napoleon and made Russia the strongest continental power. And yet he never had peace of mind. Before leaving his capital for Taganrog, he came to the Lavra to consult Father Alexis. Alexander never returned to St. Petersburg. Officially he died in Taganrog. Some people, however, believe he did not die there but left for the Holy Land, while a soldier was buried in his stead in the fortress. It is also said that he returned to Russia afterwards and died in Siberia as Staretz Feodor Kuzmich. There is a certain amount of mystery here. These reports may be only rumors, but there is no smoke without fire.

"Keep your conscience pure, Serezha, and repent as soon as you have sinned. Pray often and read the Holy Scriptures and meditate upon them. That is all I have to say to you." And with this word of life, Father closed our last conversation.

I never met Father Sergius in later years. The Lavra was closed during the revolution and the community dispersed. The Metropolitan Benjamin Kazanski was executed in the twenties, as well as some monks. Others were deported to die in concentration camps. Father Sergius disappeared in those years. In 1960 I revisited the former imperial capital, renamed Leningrad. The Lavra of Saint Alexander

Nevsky is now occupied by various Soviet institutions. There is no longer any monastic community there, though the Lavra still houses the Academy of Theology and the Seminary. And the Metropolitan still has his residence there. The Katholicon, the Church of the Holy Trinity, has been restored to worship and is filled to overflowing on Sundays and feasts. This would, indeed, be a consolation to the humble Father who had given me so much good advice.

CHAPTER 2

Staretz Basileus

I was seven years old at the most and had gone with my grand-mother, Elisavetna Alexeevna, across the bridge over the little Monastuirka river, to the Lavra of Saint Alexander Nevsky at St. Petersburg. It was winter, January, a day with sunshine but extremely cold. All of a sudden I saw an unusual figure approaching us: an elder in a blue cassock, head uncovered, with white hair and a beard. He held in his hand a long cane of ebony with the imperial crown at the top. What amazed me the most was to see the elder walking bare foot in such brisk weather. Furthermore his feet were not red or bruised, but rose colored as if he had been walking on a soft carpet. I stopped, really stunned, especially when I saw that the elder, who had noticed my grandmother, was coming directly toward us.

"Good day, highly esteemed Elisavetna Alexeevna. Are you coming to venerate the relics on such a cold day? You do well. Neither the heat nor the cold can separate us from the Lord. And this little boy with you is certainly your grandson. You have taken him with you. That's good, very good." And the stately elder left us.

"Who is he, grandmother?" I asked.

"It is the Staretz Basileus, my little one. He is a spiritual man. He is welcomed everywhere, even by the Emperor. The cane with the crown is a gift from the sovereign."

"But how can he go about bare foot? I have fur boots and a

Finnish cap and he has no gloves and his head is uncovered. How is that possible?"

"The Prayer warms him. In olden days, in the far north, the holy ascetics lived in caves and even in the hollows of trees and in intense cold. Here, in comparison it is nothing. The Prayer warmed them."

"What prayer, grandmother?"

"The prayer called the Prayer of Jesus. It is said as follows: 'Lord Jesus Christ, Son of God, have mercy upon me, a sinner.' The monks are obliged to recite this prayer in their cells but this prayer is also recommended to all the faithful. The one who practices this prayer and repeats it unceasingly warms himself. He is indifferent to heat or cold. He suffers very little from hunger or thirst. But now faith has diminished. Even in the monasteries, they are negligent in practicing it or they do it wrongly. Because of this there is not among today's monks the faith that moves mountains or heals the sick. In order that the Staretz Basileus may walk bare foot in cold weather of minus twenty degrees, he must have a strong faith and also the Prayer."

"Is it only the monks who practice this Prayer?" I asked my grandmother.

"No, not only them. Father John Sergiev, the priest of Kronstadt, is also a great man of prayer. He performs miracles and he heals the sick. There are also others, even in the world. But you are still too young and you cannot understand this now. You will understand it later. In the family of your mother, the Abbess Anfisa was highly venerated. She was a great traditionalist and she kept the ancient rituals. Monsignor Anthony, the Metropolitan of St. Petersburg and Primate of Russia, is a fine man. He was a professor and when his wife and children died he became a monk. And he is now Metropolitan. He was ninety-three years of age when he died and he was still in service. The one who fasts a great deal and who lives poorly, that one has a long life and dies well. You, you like cakes and chocolate very much. This is not good. We must not become attached to anything. Everything passes."

"What is meant by 'Everything passes'?" I asked my grandmother. "Winter and summer pass, that I know. But what else also passes?"

"Well, you had your grandfather, Avraamy Pavlovitch, and he is no more. He has passed."

Such an explanation stunned me but I was too timid to question further. We entered into the Katholikon of the Very Holy Trinity which was well lighted and well heated. My grandmother bought two candles to place them lighted before the great silver shrine of Saint Alexander Nevsky, the Grand Duke of Russia in the thirteenth century. An impressive priest-monk met us at the entrance.

"You have come here with your grandson in such cold weather, Elisavetna Alexeevna? It is praiseworthy."

"We have met the Staretz Basileus," I said. "He goes bare foot with his head uncovered and he does not feel the cold. How is that possible?"

"You are curious," the monk said with a smile. "Well, the Jesus Prayer warms him like a fur coat. He walks on snow as if he is walking on the smooth carpet of a living room. The newly canonized saint, Saint Seraphim of Sarov, spoke about this. Pray like them. Learn this Prayer and repeat it often. You will then see for yourself. For the time being you are still too young but later you must start to practice it. Otherwise you will become corrupted and you will lose the faith like our students. However, without faith, my little brother, it is impossible to live."

"My little grandson is very pious," observed my grandmother. "In his room there are many icons. A wall is full of icons. He lights the candles and lamps in front of the icons and he prays. I suppose that he takes after his great-aunt, the Abbess Anfisa."

"They are pious while they are still children," observed the priest-monk, "but once they grow up, they fall into atheism. But you,

13

Serezha, never abandon the Prayer. Pray as you can. Difficult times are approaching. We have had a Revolution. It has weakened but for the moment only. Saint Seraphim has predicted extremely difficult times for us. We will be saved only by prayer and by patience. You and I, Elisavetna Alexeevna, we will not see those horrors but the young one will certainly see them. Then the prayer will help him."

On the way back home with my grandmother I reflected upon that conversation. More than sixty years have passed now but I can still remember that morning of January 1908.

CHAPTER 3

Nanny Lyuba

Before 1914 the wealthy families were served by a numerous personnel, male and female. This was the case in my childhood. A nanny, Lyuba, looked after me and then after my younger brother. In 1908 when I was seven years old I already had a tutor but I preferred the nanny to him. Lyuba was then about twenty-five years old. She was a foundling, brought up in the Foundling's House in St. Petersburg. Lyuba was very devout and left us to enter a convent in the Diocese of Tver. She was good looking and of a rare, well-balanced character. I never saw her angry or talking ill about other people. She was a good worker and was liked and appreciated by everybody. She often read the Gospel and the lives of the saints to me.

The latter interested me very much. To such an extent that I set up a real chapel in one of my rooms with an iconostasis. Before it there were lampadas and candles, which I lit before praying. I would use a proper prayer book. My prayers deeply touched the nanny.

"Pray, Serezha," she used to say, "perhaps one day you will enter a monastery as I am about to do. In the world, Serezha, there is only unhappiness and tears, vanity of vanities. But in the monastery it is like being in heaven. Where the Church is, there is true heaven. But even if the Lord God does not call you to religious life you can live as a true Christian in the world. Never neglect prayer, Serezha."

My mother, who greatly appreciated Lyuba, used to tell her occasionally: "Lyuba, it is time for you to marry. We shall find a good man for you. You should be pleased."

Once, when my mother said that, Lyuba answered quietly: "Madam, I have decided to enter a nunnery. I am a foundling. My only hope is God. Besides, I am attracted to that life."

My mother became thoughtful. "Yes, you are right, Lyuba. If the Lord calls you, go on. The sister of my grandmother, Anna, a beautiful young woman with a large dowry, and clever too, decided to enter the cloister. Later she became the Abbess. I met her in my childhood. I shall regret losing you but perhaps it is for the good. No one knows what kind of husband you would have, perhaps a drunkard or a hard man. In the convent you will be well looked after. I shall tell all this to my husband and we shall give you a proper dowry. You will be received properly and not like a penniless foundling."

"Why, Madam," Lyuba answered, "I am ready to enter as I am now. I am accustomed to work. Besides, it is humbler."

"No, Lyuba. None of our female servants left us without a dowry on marrying. You are the first to go to the convent. You will pray for us. Prayer is needed. I am rather unwell now. So, it is decided. You will leave us as a daughter. We shall invite the Abbess here to arrange the formalities. Your dowry will be substantial."

Two years later, a very dignified Abbess visited us. She dined with my parents and they remained discussing various things for quite a long time. Then a few days later my mother said to me: "Well, Serezha, everything is arranged. We gave Lyuba a proper dowry. The Mother Abbess was very much touched and said: 'Rare are the parents who give so much for their daughters as you did for Lyuba. For the community she will be a treasure: modest, quiet, a good worker and a fine voice. She will sing in the choir. We lack a real contralto.'"

On the fourth week of Lent we said our farewell to Lyuba.

According to the custom she asked forgiveness from all of us. My younger brother cried and I was very much troubled myself. Our coachman drove her to Nikolaevsky Station. Lyuba was accompanied by Masha, one of our maids, to see how Lyuba was received and to remain in the convent for a week. Lyuba's convent pleased Masha very much. "The nuns are very nice and they received Lyuba very kindly," she reported on her return.

Lyuba wrote to my mother quite often, even after the Bolshevik Revolution. Then my mother died in 1918. The following year I left Russia in the midst of the Civil War. What happened to Lyuba, I do not know. I heard her monastery was closed by the Communists in 1925. By 1936 no monastery remained open in Russia. They only reappeared after the Second World War.

I always remember Lyuba as someone serene and kind.

CHAPTER 4

My Mother, Lydia Bolshakoff

In May 1918, two months before the death of my mother, I had a long talk with her. She was asking me about the ceremony of the consecration of Father Simon Shleev as Bishop of the Edinovertsy. Tikhon, Patriarch of Moscow and all Russia, had been the principal consecrator. Although my mother was barely forty and looked ten years younger, she was condemned to die quickly and she knew her fate.

"I have not visited the Lavra of St. Alexander Nevsky, where Father Simon was consecrated, for some time," my mother said sadly. "And I don't expect to revisit it. My end is near. I used to visit the Lavra often as a girl. My compatriot, Fr. Pallady Raev, was Metropolitan there in the 1890's. He died the year of my wedding, 1898. He had been priest in Nizhny-Novgorod on the Volga and he taught in the seminary. He was a married man, his life was happy and he expected to end his life in his native city. Suddenly his wife died in 1860, while she was still quite young. The following year he entered monastic life. Handsome, wise, a fine preacher, he was soon noticed and promoted. Within six years he was made auxiliary bishop to Metropolitan Isidor, then Primate of Russia in St. Petersburg. At the time of his consecration Bishop Pallady said: 'We should live, not according to our own will and taste but according to the will of God and our duty.' In 1892 returning to the Lavra of St. Alexander as Primate of Russia, Metropolitan Pallady said to the community, who came to meet him: 'God directs our steps and the Lord puts everyone in his proper place.'

"You, Serezha, are just beginning your independent life. Now we live in the midst of a revolution with all its terror and civil strife. The Lord only knows what will happen next. We shall go within a fortnight to my birthplace, to the province of Nizhny-Novgorod. It is very likely that I shall not return here but will be buried with my parents in Zhelnino.

"From Tchernoe you may visit some monasteries at the Kerzhenetz. Your great-aunt, the Abbess Anfisa, is buried there. I visited her with my parents as a small girl. Later I visited the lake of Svetly Yar in the Makariev forests. According to the old legend the Grand Duke of Vladimir, George Vsevolodovich, constructed near Lake Svetly Yar the city of Great Kitiesh with its many churches and two monasteries. That was at the beginning of the thirteenth century. A couple of decades later the Mongols of Genghis Khan, commanded by his grandson Batu Khan, invaded Russia. The Grand Duke retreated to Great Kitiesh. When Batu Khan approached that city it became invisible. It will reappear when Orthodoxy shines again as in the past. The same legend teaches us how to enter Kitiesh in the present day. He who wants to enter the invisible city, must leave behind all worldly cares and ambitions and, without looking to right or to left, fearless of devils, go to the lake by the path of Batu.

"I believe Kitiesh is the inner chamber in our heart which we should try to penetrate in order to venerate God in spirit and truth. Into this invisible Kitiesh no foe can enter if we live with the prayer of heart and devotion. A nun of Kerzhenetz told me so. The lake is very beautiful and silent, except in summer, when the pilgrims come.

"There is also another mysterious lake, called Nestiar, where, according to the legend, there is an invisible monastery, inhabited by seven saintly startzy. They are unknown to the sinful world but revealed to those who are really devout and pray earnestly. These great startzy live even now but the world cannot see them because it lies in evil. Nevertheless, if a person repents and lives according to the Gospel, the same startzy will reveal themselves to that person who searches for them — often in places where he does not expect to find them. One can look and not see, listen and not understand. When you receive spiritual understanding, you will find those startzy, Serezha."

My mother died at the end of July in 1918 in the province of Nizhny-Novgorod, which is now called Gorki, but I never forgot our talk on that May afternoon.

She was right. I found these startzy to be the true masters of the Prayer of the Heart.

CHAPTER 5

Grandmother Maria Nikolaevna

My mother died on July 20, 1918, during the second year of the Soviet Revolution, in her native place at Tchernoe. She was buried in the tomb of her family, the Balounine, at Zhelnino. She was in her early forties when she died. She had contracted tuberculosis when she was thirty years old and later on developed a cardiac condition. The tragedy of my mother lay in the fact that she, who was a beautiful and rich woman, had to suffer and endure sickness instead of enjoying her life in this world. My mother was a very pious woman. She observed the fasts and she prayed according to the ancient ritual, which was longer and more complicated than the one commonly employed at that time. I am much indebted to my mother for my own personal piety.

My grandmother, her mother, Maria Nikolaevna Balounine was in 1918 well over sixty years of age. She was majestic, authoritarian and severe, but also fair. She was an enemy of falsehood and she was pious like my mother. Her life, especially in the first years of her marriage, had been difficult. She was married while still young to a man much older than herself. He was a widower with children. He was authoritarian and also irascible. But slowly the young woman became the real governor of the house, well respected by all.

One evening, a few days after the death of my mother, I was sitting on the balcony of our beautiful home. The scenery was magnificent: the wide and deep river Oka and beyond it the distant mountains. "You are sad, Serezha," observed my grandmother as she approached me. "Instead of being sad, you should rejoice."

"Why, grandmother?"

"Your mother is now where there is no sickness, no sadness, no sighing. She died as a good Christian and she is buried near her father. Her life as a wife and mother was a model for all to see. Therefore, everything is fine. God called her at the right time. With wars both at home and abroad, difficult times are approaching. She would suffer greatly if she were still alive. With God it is not as it is for us. His ways are incomprehensible and they always lead to what is best for us. With age we understand these things better.

"When I was your age, a young girl of seventeen years, I went one day with my mother to the Skete of Kerzhenetz for the solemn profession of my cousin and friend, Lenotchka. I still remember very well that pilgrimage. It was on a beautiful day in spring, after Easter. Some small white clouds floated across the blue sky. Delicate birch trees bordered the path that led to the Skete. All around were the great forests of Kerzhenetz, the cottages of the nuns and their gardens. All this was illumined by the sun, not the meridian sun, but like the sun in Nesterov's painting *Solemn Profession*. As in this well-known painting, the procession went forward: first, the newly professed, beautiful and serene, followed by the novices and then the older nuns, solemnly and silently. Her kinswoman, aunt of my future husband, was then the Abbess. I felt so good that I thought that I would stay there to live in peace and silence. But the Lord had predestined me to marry a widower who was hard and irritable. And he had four children, all still young. While blessing me before my departure for the wedding ceremonies at church, my mother told me: 'Machenka, you now marry a very rich widower, a hard man with four small children, and you are not yet nineteen. You will no doubt be obliged to suffer much and to pass through great hardships, but remain faithful to your duty and remember that work and patience take care of all obstacles.' And that is what really happened. Never did I regret that life could have been different for me if I had married another man, young and good. I recommend that you should do the same as me. Always remember the text of the Scriptures: *Be faithful until death and I will give you the crown of life.* They have just informed me that our sovereign, Czar Nicholas Alexandrovitch, has been shot at Ekaterinburg with all his family and all his entourage. Since the time of troubles, three hundred years ago, such a crime has not occurred in Russia. In the past, the times of troubles have lasted until all the killers and traitors have exterminated one another. It will be the same thing now. In a normal period, you would have been a rich man and would have lived with riches and honors. This Revolution, or rather the Lord, deprives you of all this. Do not regret it. In exchange, you will receive great spiritual liberty that will not be hindered by all these properties, businesses and factories."

"And what advice would you give me, grandmother, if the Revolution becomes even more radical, and if all the properties are lost for ever?"

"I have already told you. Live according to your conscience and do not deviate from it ever for a higher position or for a better income. Those who do that receive for their reward irritability, worries about their own possessions, honors, intrigues, humiliations at the hands of those who are powerful in this world, envy in regards to the happiness of rivals. And if someone had resorted to crime to obtain the things desired, the situation becomes even worse. In reality one harvests what one has sown. The one who has sown good will harvest good and the one who has sown evil will reap evil. The times of godlessness approach, but you, do not look to others. Remain faithful and you will never be put to shame. Pray like Abbess Anfisa. Even when she was well past seventy years old, she still stood up as straight as a candle and she did all the metanias. She died at ninety after a beautiful old age, neither deaf nor blind nor paralyzed. And she died well, she simply fell asleep after a long life full of good deeds. Even so, the main thing is not the metanias and the prostrations but a pure heart and a clear conscience."

23

Part II

Estonia

In 1926 the author spent three summer months at the well-known Pskovo-Petchersky Monastery in Estonia. There he had meetings with "some wise and good monks." In Part Two there are accounts of his talks with four of them and also with two laymen.

CHAPTER 6

Father Theophan

The university town of Tartu, in Estonia, where I lived for a few years after I left Russia in 1919, was founded in 1030 by Yaroslav the Wise, Grand Duke of Russia. In 1224 it was seized by German knights and renamed Dorpat. Some Russian merchants and artisans, however, remained in the town and formed two parishes. The relations between the Russians and the Germans were variable but on the whole satisfactory. Although two Crusades were preached to subdue the Russian Orthodox and make them Latins, they were both unsuccessful and did not embitter the mutual relations unduly. The Swedes were routed near modern Leningrad on July 15, 1240 by Saint Alexander Nevsky, Grand Duke of Russia. Then on April 5, 1242 he destroyed the German Crusaders on the ice covering Lake Peipus in Estonia. Six years later, Pope Innocent IV sent two legates to Saint Alexander, urging him to join the Roman Church, but the embassy came to naught. The memories of the Fourth Crusade and the sacking of Constantinople by the Latins in 1204 were yet too fresh in the minds of the Orthodox.

After the final failure of the Swedes to subdue the Russians a century later, relations were stabilized and became even friendly. The Latins were allowed to have churches and monasteries in several commercial cities of the Russian North, such as Novgorod, Pskov and Ladoga. Some Latin monks even helped Archbishop Gennadius

27

of Novgorod (1485-1505) to combat the Judaizers. This was an heretical sect that practiced Jewish rites. It appeared in Russia in the fifteenth century. The Archbishop needed a complete Slavonic translation of the Old Testament to confound the heretics. As he was unable to obtain complete Greek or Slavonic Bibles, he was obliged to make his translation from the Vulgate. It was the Dominican Friar Benjamin, a Slovene by extraction, who, with the help of his nephew, did this for the Archbishop, translating some books of the Old Testament from the Vulgate in 1493. The Bible of Archbishop Gennadius was the only Slavonic Bible in Russia until Prince Constantine Ostrogski published another in 1580. In his edition the Prince retained much from the Bible of Gennadius. As a result, up to the present time the Russian Church still uses at its services a Bible some books of which were translated from the Vulgate by the Dominican Friar Benjamin. The Friar also wrote for the Archbishop a long sermon against those who oppress the Church.

Sometimes, however, relations with the Latins were disturbed by local incidents. The story of Tartu is one of them. Although by the Treaty of 1443 the Latin Bishop of Dorpat had agreed to allow the Russians to keep two parishes of their rite in the city, he in fact so oppressed them that one parish soon closed, and its priest, Father John, retired to the Russian principality of Pskov. There he took up his abode near the grotto where a solitary, Saint Mark, had lived. When the wife of Father John became a nun, he, too, entered the religious life and founded a monastery later known as the Pskovo-Petchersky Monastery. Its monastic church was consecrated on August 15, 1477. Meanwhile the pastor of the remaining Russian parish in Tartu, Father Isidore, was arrested with seventy-two companions by order of the Latin Prince-Bishop. They were all drowned on January 8, 1472 because of their refusal to accept the Latin rite. Isidore was canonized as a martyr and a chapel was dedicated to him in the collegiate church of Tartu. By a strange coincidence there is also a chapel there dedicated to Saint Josaphat Kunzevich, a well-known martyr for union with Rome, who died in White Russia during the seventeenth century. The Tartu incident was finally settled peacefully and a new treaty restored to the Russians their former privileges.

Pskovo-Petchersky Monastery developed very slowly but in time became fully established.

The deep, solemn tone of the abbey bell roused me from sleep, refreshed and joyful. The air was pure and invigorating. Drops of dew sparkled like diamonds on the grass, the leaves and the flowers. In the sunshine of the early morning, against the background of a pale blue sky and verdant trees, the cream-white buildings with their many domes and campaniles rose before me like a fantasy. Everything was ethereal, full of unearthly beauty. Holy Russia lived again. I was taken back to the days of its glory. All things unpleasant, even the war, revolutions and exile disappeared like smoke on that autumn day. For me the Pskovo-Petchersky Monastery was a true Kitiesh — the legendary town in northern Russia that disappeared in a lake when the Mongolians besieged it in the thirteenth century. The Holy Lake is still there amid the Volga forests and, according to the legend, a man with a pure heart may find the entrance to the city. I found the entrance to my own Kitiesh.

In the old Katholicon, carved in the rock of the hill, the monks arranged themselves in a semicircle before the venerated icon of Our Lady. The Hegumen-Bishop stood in the center.

"Blessed be the Kingdom of the Father and of the Son and of the Holy Ghost," intoned the celebrant with a strong, solemn voice. Prayers and hymns alternated. The monks sang well, using old melodies similar to those of Western plain-chant. Each word of the psalms was uttered clearly and slowly, and the mind willingly followed in joyful meditation. After the service, Father Vassian, the confessor of the community, began the celebration of the Liturgy. On that "Kitiesh" morning, I realized for the first time the deep mystical beauty of the Liturgy, although I had participated in it hundreds of times before. As I contemplated the solemn rites, I sensed beneath them the mysteries of Calvary and the Resurrection. The fine old church, the carved and gilded iconostasis, the delicately embroidered seventeenth-century vestments, the heavenly singing, made the whole celebration extraordinarily beautiful. I beheld the venerable priest. His grey eyes mirrored visions of glory accessible only to contemplatives.

In the afternoon, Brother Sergius showed me the numberless wonders of the monastery: its churches and chapels, its sacristy and library, its cells and catacombs, its towers and gardens. I was impressed most of all by the monastic catacombs or grottoes — long galleries in the rock behind the old Katholicon. Carved in the sandstone, they are broad, high and airy. Many thousands of monks and a few laymen are buried there. The coffins are usually placed in an excavation in the wall, which is then sealed with a tablet on which is engraved the name of the deceased and the date of his death. In a small chapel near the entrance there are three sarcophagi, enshrining the relics of Saints Mark, Jonas, and Vassa. Another chapel, deep in the rock, contains the coffins of several hegumens and recluses, including that of Father Theodosius, the last occupant of my cell. The coffins rested directly on the floor and were covered with a pall. A solemn, comforting silence reigned in this chapel deep within the rock. The air was fresh and pure, with a faint aroma of violets. The candles burned quietly. Under the purple velvet palls, in plain oak coffins, slept the Servants of God. The horror of death was absent; there was no nauseating odor, no terrifying mask on the faces of the dead. Whenever these coffins have been opened, the bodies of the Servants of God have been found intact, their faces serene and venerable. It is difficult to describe the atmosphere of this chapel. One feels transported to another world, entirely different from this world of ours, one that is radiant and peaceful.

I first met Father Theophan in Pskovo-Petchersky Monastery in 1926. He was then about seventy years old. A peasant from the province of Pskov, he had become a widower early in life but did not remarry. After seeing his only daughter married to a peasant from the same district and leaving all his property to her, the widower retired to Pskovo-Petchersky Monastery, where in due course he was professed under the name of Theophan. He was a very good monk. He loved prayer and work. For humility's sake he declined being prepared for ordination.

When my friend Father Isaya Bobinin entered the Pskovo-Petchersky Monastery, he and Father Theophan became close friends and often met to discuss questions of spirituality. They had much in common: a peasant background, a love for reading, and piety. Father Isaya introduced me to Father Theophan and we met often, usually in the garden of the monastery. Father Theophan loved to read, especially the writings of Bishop Theophan the Recluse. I believe it was in honor of the Recluse that he received the monastic name of Theophan.

Once when I was conversing with the old monk in the garden he said: "Well, Sergei Nikolaevitch, the most important activity in life is unceasing prayer. We must pray always: when we rise, when we walk, when we eat, always, on every occasion. And we must pray with attention and feeling. To every appeal to pray we should say within ourselves: 'My heart is ready.' And we should not stop praying until our hunger is satisfied. Our whole life should be a continuous prayer. For every activity there is a proper time, but for prayer the time is always, just as for breathing. Our prayer and breathing should be united: every breath a prayer. I speak of the Prayer of the Heart, of which Father Isaya told you."

"That is the Prayer of Jesus?"

"It is. But we may very well compose our own short prayers, as did Saint Tikhon of Zadonsk. For example: Lord, teach me! Lord, give me understanding! Lord, help me! And we should do this in fear and trembling. Especially should we thank and glorify God for the greatness and richness of his mercy. We should beg for understanding of how to live according to the Divine will; if we do, it will be revealed to us. To ask for wealth, power, honors, or things of that kind would be to create idols. It is better not to ask for a wife or children or health or a long life, because we do not know if such things are good for us. Nor should we persist in asking if the Lord does not give us what we have requested for a long time. If we persist, the Lord might grant our request to our own sorrow. If the Lord does not grant our request it may mean that what we ask for would be harmful to ourselves or to others. The only thing we should ask for persistently is stated in the Our Father: Thy will be done."

At that moment a monk appeared in the distance, slowly coming our way.

"Who is he?" I asked.

"That is Father Vassian, our community's confessor," he answered, "a true staretz, though he is younger than I. True wisdom is acquired not by a long life but by life in Christ. So it is with Father Vassian. He came to us when still quite young. Though he is now a hieromonk and our community confessor, Father Vassian, like the Apostle Paul, works with his own hands. Some monks believe that if one becomes a hieromonk one is excused from hard manual labor and his business is to command other people. But this is not so."

Father Theophan went on to relate this story: "Filaret Amfiteatrov, Metropolitan of Kiev, was a member of the Holy Synod and the recipient of the Grand Cross of Saint Andrew and other distinctions. He was even received into the Imperial Family. But he experienced many sorrows in his life. He was persecuted by those who disliked his ascetic ways and his stand for truth. Yet he never complained. His innocence was recognized and he was rapidly promoted.

"One time when he traveled from Kiev to St. Petersburg to attend a session of the Holy Synod, the Metropolitan was crossing the province of Kursk. As was customary in those days, when railways were rare, he traveled in a coach with an escort. On the way, the Metropolitan wanted to visit a monastery about which he had heard a great deal. Because his heavy coach moved very slowly, Metropolitan Filaret went ahead alone in a peasant cart, dressed as usual as a simple monk, without any sign of his dignity. He arrived at the monastery just as the early Liturgy was beginning in the church. It was sung, on this occasion, in a side chapel. There were only a few people present, among them an important-looking hieromonk. When the time came for the Little Entrance with the Gospel text, there was no one to carry the candle before the priest. The Metropolitan turned to the hieromonk and said: 'Father, take the candle and walk before the priest.' The dignified hieromonk answered coolly: 'I am a hieromonk and not an acolyte. Go and carry the candle yourself.' The Metropolitan obeyed and walked before the celebrant with the candle.

"At the end of the service there was a commotion in the church. The archimandrite came in, dressed as for a great occasion, followed by the senior members of his Synod. They all went directly to the Metropolitan and welcomed him according to custom. The pompous hieromonk realized then that the "monk" he had haughtily told to function as acolyte was the Metropolitan of Kiev! He was much abashed, but the Metropolitan in his kindness said nothing."

While Father Theophan was narrating this incident, Father Vassian arrived. "The Lord bless you, friends," he said, taking his seat on the bench. "What are you speaking about?"

Father Theophan answered: "I am telling Sergei Nikolaevitch here that we must strive to pray always and with humility."

"You do well to discuss spiritual things and not judge others. Alas, because of our sins, even in monasteries we often fail and begin to make judgments that are reserved to the Lord alone."

The staretz then took up Father Theophan's theme: "It is true, we must pray with prudence and confidence, asking for nothing worldly. The Lord knows better than we do what is useful for us. We must surrender ourselves to Divine Providence always and everywhere. This is true wisdom. The longer I live the more I see how the Lord guides us at all times, leading us toward good and holy things and destroying in us everything earthly and all our evil inclinations. In order to pray with attention we must preserve a fear of God. He who always keeps in mind his death and the judgment of Christ will not sin easily. All this is very simple."

"Your monastery is idiorrhythmic, Father Vassian," I observed. "Valaam is truly cenobitic, is it not?"

"That is true, Sergei Nikolaevitch. Because of our sins we are surrounded by a world of vanities. When monks have money of their own it is difficult to avoid envy and the love of material things. Yet even here it is possible to attain salvation. We also have had blessed startzy. There was Father Lazar, with whom Alexander I corresponded, and later Staretz Theodosius, whose cell you now occupy."

Father then gave his teaching: "One can be saved anywhere and one can also perish anywhere. Satan was the highest angel, standing always before God and yet he fell by pride. Judas the Iscariot was one of the twelve Apostles and yet because of his love for money he betrayed the Lord and afterward committed suicide. A good many people have perished in like manner. On the other hand, the sinful publican was justified by one short prayer. The good thief, already crucified, was saved, too, by one short prayer and entered paradise together with the Lord Himself. Our Lord told the proud, avaricious Scribes and Pharisees that the publicans and the whores would go into the Kingdom of God before them because they repented at the preaching of Saint John the Baptist whereas the proud teachers did not."

"But penance must be not only in words but in deeds as well, Father Vassian?"

"Of course. We are saved by deeds and not merely by words. The Savior himself once said: 'These people come to me saying: "Lord, Lord," but their heart is far from me.' Certainly, according to Saint Paul, it is impossible to please God without faith but we must not forget Saint James who asserted that faith without works is dead and that even the devils believe and tremble but they do nothing of merit."

"Father Vassian," I said, "many people nowadays assert that devils do not exist and that we sin only because of our own defects and passions."

"Yes, people who are supposed to be learned often say things like that, but they are truly unwise." Then Father shared more of his wisdom: "Devils always try to persuade their victims that they do not exist because if they do not exist it is useless to struggle with them. We can then rest easy with our defects and passions and even be condescending towards them, arguing that they are ingrained in us, inseparable from our perverted nature. Whether devils exist or not, we can learn by personal experience. Only try to lead a truly Christian life and temptations and troubles of all kinds will assail you. It is true, as wise men say, that there is a devil assigned to every Christian to tempt him; but to a monk, two are assigned. Devils seduce us to sin by filling our imaginations with daydreams and fantasies. Satan dreamed of being equal to God and fell. Likewise Judas. We must avoid, at all cost, daydreaming and laziness. While working, we must occupy our mind with the Prayer of Jesus. If we do this, devils find no place near us and we need not fear them. They are not all-powerful.

"It is also true that a heart completely free of daydreams and fantasies gives birth to thoughts both divine and mysterious which play about in it as dolphins in a still, sunbathed sea.

"Well, friends, I must go on my way," Father Vassian said as he rose and quietly started down the path.

"How right he is, dear Sergei Nikolaevitch," Father Theophan observed. And he added his own thoughts: "We must be afraid of all daydreams, fantasies and illusions and fill our heart with the invocation of the Divine Name. And yet we all dream, always waiting for something, even in our old age. The young dream all the time. They dream of having a prosperous life, full of pleasures, honors, riches and power. And in order to attain such a life they resort to lies and flattery and become hard and cruel. There are, of course, many exceptions, but such is the rule. Do you know, Sergei Nikolaevitch, that old age is better than youth? And why? Because it is wiser. In old age we realize at last that all is vanity. 'Vanity of vanities and all things are vanity,' as Ecclesiastes says. Everything passes away: our youth, our health, our relatives and our friends, our foes, our wealth and our honors. Only peace of mind, good deeds, and eternity remain."

Father Theophan died a few years after I left Pskovo-Petchersky

Monastery. His end was peaceful, without suffering, without a struggle. Father Vassian became a megaloschemos, receiving the name Symeon. He died at the ripe old age of ninety-three, a couple of years before my visit to Pskovo-Petchersky Monastery in 1960. He sang the Liturgy daily and worked in his shop till the very end. They told me he died without any suffering; he just fell asleep to wake in another world.

It may not always be easy to live as a monk but to die as a monk, a good monk who has seen the great Light and walked in His radiance — that is true blessedness.

CHAPTER 7

Father Vassian

I met Father Vassian for the first time in June 1926 in Pskovo-Petchersky Monastery, then in Estonia. On the first morning after my arrival at the monastery I went to the early Liturgy, celebrated at five o'clock in the morning. The sun was already above the hills surrounding the monastery. The air was pure and invigorating. In the blue cloudless sky the birds sang their morning concert. Around me, encircling the monastic court, stood several churches, white, green and rose, with their bulbous domes decorated with golden stars. The bells sounded gravely.

I entered the old Abbey-Church of the Dormition, built into the hill. It was cool and in semidarkness. The morning service began. The monks sang and read clearly and well. The office lasted for a long time. Then after kissing the icon on the shrine of Saint Cornelius, an Abbot of Pskovo-Petchersky in the sixteenth century, the monks went off to their various works and duties. Only those celebrating and serving the Liturgy remained. Father Vassian, vested in a rich chasuble of fiery red velvet embroidered with pearls, incensed the high altar. The blue clouds of the incense melding with the perfume of the flowering lilac in the garden produced an unusual and pleasant aroma.

The founders and deceased benefactors were commemorated at length: "We pray for the rest of the souls of the most pious Sovereign Czars, John Vassilievitch, Theodore Joannovich, Boris Theodorovitch,... and of the Saintly Patriarchs of All Russia, Job, Joseph, Joasaph...." Russian history revived in the old church.

The attending Bishop, John Bulin, and the cantor started to sing the Hymn of the Cherubim. Father Vassian came out of the sanctuary with the Holy Gifts to be consecrated. The Liturgy proceeded slowly and solemnly. There were a few communicants and we ended with the Thanksgiving service.

When I left the church Bishop John, young and handsome, just thirty, invited me to join him for a talk. Father Vassian passed us, making the customary low bow. "What is the name of the celebrating priest, my Lord?", I asked the Bishop. "Father Vassian," the latter answered. "He is our confessor. He is a very good monk. Make friends with him."

A few days later I met Father Vassian in the upper garden of the monastery. It was a beautiful and sunny June day. Through the greenery of the mighty trees one could see the deep blue sky, radiant with sunshine. The perfumed air was warm.

"What a beautiful day!" was Father Vassian's opening greeting. "Yes, the feast of Saints Peter and Paul is near. Do you come here for a longish stay, man of God? What is your name, my friend?"

"Sergei Nikolaevitch," I answered.

"But what Sergei is your patron? A martyr, or a confessor? And if the latter who is he, that of Radonezh or of Valaam?"

"Of Radonezh."

"That is good. The godless rulers of Russia have now suppressed the great Lavra founded by Saint Sergei in the fourteenth century. So far we are open. Valaam still exists too."

"Why did all that happen, Father Vassian, I mean the Bolshevik Revolution? All those troubles and disorders?"

"It is very simple, brother Sergei. People fell into the vanity of vanities, abandoned God and thereby lost their reason. The Scripture says: 'Without God you cannot cross the threshold, but with Him you are safe to go over seas.'"

"But why did people abandon God and fall into vanity, Father Vassian?"

"Because we abandoned prayer and fasting. Without prayer and ascetic life you cannot keep up faith. Faith is revealed in deeds, my friend. Without them it is dead, merely an abstract idea." So ended our first conversation.

Our second talk took place in the beehive garden, one warm summer evening. We were four: Father Pimen, the sacristan; Father Vassian; Father Isaya, the beekeeper and myself. Father Isaya liked to complain about the degeneration of contemporary monasticism which took place after his spiritual master Bishop Ignatius Brianchaninov died in 1867. The latter reproached his contemporary monks because they forgot the practice of the Prayer of the Heart and were satisfied with the scrupulous observance of rites, long offices and so on. Because piety became mostly external, fine singing and reading, monastic life became external too. Father Isaya repeated all this that particular morning.

"It depends how we read and how we sing," Father Vassian observed. "If we read and sing with attention, feelingly and humbly, then the offices are very useful. On the other hand, if we practice the Jesus Prayer without due attention and devotion, merely repeating that prayer as many times as possible, we sin gravely and that very prayer might become an obstacle to our spiritual progress. The Startzy of Optino warned us against that failing. We shouldn't criticize other people, how they read and sing. We must look at ourselves. Now the lime trees are blooming and the bees are all around them. This may teach us how to progress in the spiritual life.

"When our soul is full of virtues it attracts people looking for inner peace. The responsibility of the confessor is, therefore, to sanctify himself first and then he will know how to sanctify other people. We all need spiritual experience. School theology isn't enough. It is only theory. We need also experience. I must go away, brethren," Father Vassian said, rising. "Forgive me, if I said something painful. There is no salvation in talkativeness. Often we are bold enough to teach other people while neglecting to look after ourselves. The Staretz Ambrose of Optino truly said at the end of his life: 'I covered the houses of other people with roofs but my own is still unroofed.'"

On one occasion before leaving the monastery to go abroad, after the great ceremonies of the 450th anniversary of Pskovo-Petchersky, I said to Father Vassian: "What splendid ceremonies, what fine singing we had here lately, Father."

"Yes," he answered thoughtfully, "but all that is external; helpful of course, but not enough. We must build the temple of God within ourselves, within our heart, where the Lord God himself is present, and to him we must offer continually our sacrifice of prayer of mind and heart. When we construct this inner temple then the external temple, offices and singing, touch us and bring forth fruit. But if our heart is empty, then all the external offices cannot help. They become merely concerts of religious music. This is not bad but not enough. Our chief care should be the construction of the inner temple. Within our heart there is the Kingdom of God, as the Fathers teach. Therefore we must seek the latter, all else will come in consequence. The Renovators among the clergy in Russia nowadays, instead of looking for the Kingdom of God within us, seek externally, trying to change the present structure of the Church with their reforms of rites and canons. When Christians live in peace and concord, then the canons are little talked about but when the Church is assailed with heresies and schisms, then people talk much about the canons, rules, reforms and so on. This all means that the spiritual life of the Church is at a low ebb."

Father Vassian died after the Second World War when well over ninety, keeping his health and mental clarity right to the end.

CHAPTER 8

Archdeacon Arkadi

Father Arkadi was standing on the balcony of his cell, feeding the pigeons. He was a handsome, tall man in his fifties. He was a man always in a good mood and very friendly.

"Tell me, Father Arkadi, how is it that you are always in such a good frame of mind?"

Father Arkadi answered with a smile: "And why should I be sad? I am in good health, well-fed, clothed, with shoes on my feet. I live in a good cell. I serve the Church as deacon. I work as a carpenter in the workshop of the monastery. I read devotional books and I practice the Prayer. What more is needed? According to the Apostle Paul, those who desire more expose themselves to much grief and passions. They are the slaves, sometimes of avarice, sometimes of vengeance, sometimes of carnal desires, sometimes of lust for power. When they cannot obtain the objects of their covetousness, they become rude and irritable. Nearing their end, they become worried and anxious of losing the things obtained. Therefore they are always unhappy. You, Sergei Nikolaevitch, if you desire to preserve serenity of soul, live simply, without intrigue, and everything will go well. Staretz Ambrose of Optino often said: 'Live simply, and you will live until you are a hundred years old.'"

"It is possible in a monastery, but how about in the world?"

41

"Father Ambrose added: 'One can so live in the world, but in a hidden manner, without making oneself known.'"

"But if we sin, what must we do?" "It is simple, Sergei Nikolaevitch. There is a saying of the Desert Fathers concerning this point:

> One day, a young monk came to see an elder and asked him: 'What must I do, Father? I fall continually in the same sin.'
> The elder replied: 'If you fall into sin, get up and do penance.'
> 'And if I fall again?'
> 'Then, get up and repent of your sin again.'
> 'But until when?'
> 'Until your death.'

"This is the secret, Sergei Nikolaevitch, of living serenely. There is not a man in the world without sin. The Apostle John the Theologian also wrote on this subject. But for every sin there is penitence. This same penitence saves us unceasingly, in one way, from pride and from a haughty spirit, and in another way, from despair."

"I suppose, Father Arkadi, that the Jesus Prayer is very appropriate in these circumstances. We repeat unceasingly: 'Lord, have mercy; Kyrie eleison!'"

"It is true, my brother Sergei. We sin not only at every hour but at every minute, by words, by actions and by thoughts. We easily accept *prilogs*, that is, idle, doubtful, impure, blasphemous thoughts. We examine them from all sides. Often we are in agreement with them and if we do not actually fall into sin it is simply because we do not have the occasion at hand. The Jesus Prayer is very much recommended in these situations. If a blasphemous thought rises up in your mind or if you have a carnal desire or if you would like to say something disagreeable to your neighbor or even to hit him, turn towards the Jesus Prayer.

"Say softly, or mentally: *Lord Jesus Christ, Son of God, have mercy upon me, a sinner*. Say this slowly, with attention and contrition, and these evil thoughts will leave you. If you happen to accept these thoughts and fall, do not despair, but continually repeat the same prayer. Then you will become peaceful in spirit. Before you sin the demons represent God to us as being merciful and forgiving all. They even suggest, for example, that if a man, being young and strong, sometimes falls into carnal sin, God will forgive easily. It is natural. But after you sin the demons portray God to us as a severe judge, without mercy, in order to bring us to despair. Thus they push certain scrupulous people to madness and even to suicide. On the other hand, the one who constantly asks forgiveness of God remains humble and peaceful.

"Saint Anthony the Great once saw the earth covered by diabolic traps and snares. Terrified, he asked God: 'How can one be saved?' This reply came to him: 'By humility.' That is the reason why it is so important to repeat unceasingly the Jesus Prayer. Many, even monks, say that this prayer is superfluous and say that it is enough to attend Church services and say private prayers in the cell. However, we are not always in church or in our cells and temptations still pursue us everywhere. Furthermore, if the reading and the chanting of hymns at services could save us then, as Staretz Basileus of Poliano-Merulya wrote, all readers and chanters would be models of virtue. We can see very well that this is not the case. Even if they chant very well and read admirably, their attention is rather focused on the music and the readings as such. Singing musically and reading dramatically like artists is their goal, not being attentive to the contents of the texts chanted or read. Of course, there are some chanters and readers who are truly spiritual."

"Tell me, Father Arkadi, which life is the most perfect? The active life of those in a community or the purely contemplative life of one living in a hermitage or skete?"

"For each way there is a time. The young must go into a community in order to be polished. We all know that the rocks on the shore of the sea or of a lake have rough, sharp edges until they fall into the water. There, by rubbing one against another, they become polished and become round like balls or eggs. The community acts in the same manner. It teaches us humility, patience, meekness, generosity. Once all of these virtues have been attained, then at a certain age, towards the fifties, one can begin to approach the solitary life. Before that time it is often fantasy, vanity or a high opinion of our self which guides us. But the one who is already well polished and has long experience of the Jesus Prayer can and must tend towards the solitary life and must prepare himself for the passage to a different world, the spiritual world. *For I judge the man according to the state in which I find him.*

"According to the Scriptures, the one who, like the wise virgins, is always ready, has the oil, that is the Jesus Prayer, for the lamp of his soul. He passes to the other world, prepared when he is called. In the litanies, we pray to obtain such an end: *A Christian ending of our life, painless, blameless, peaceful and a good defense before the dread judgment seat of Christ.* Such is the Jesus Prayer. The one who practices it correctly is always humble, simple, generous, good. What more could we desire?"

It was a beautiful summer morning. The golden crosses of the white, rose, and cream churches shone in the blue sky. Birds were singing in the delicate greenery of the northern trees. A joyful peace reigned everywhere.

CHAPTER 9

Father Isaya Bobinin

Shortly after my arrival at the Pskovo-Petchersky Monastery in June 1926, my friend Novice Sergei Mironovitch Paul brought to my cell a very lively little hierodeacon, Father Isaya. Father was about forty at the time. His black hair made his brilliant, intelligent eyes even more striking. I have never forgotten that first meeting.

Father Isaya was of peasant origin, coming from Novgorod Province. Influenced by his grandmother and another old peasant he early became attracted to religious life. The lives of holy monks, which were told and retold, impressed him and he wanted to imitate them. Passing pilgrims told him of the monasteries they had visited and this greatly increased his interest.

When Father Isaya reached eighteen his parents gave him their blessing to enter the strict Novgorodian monastery of the Desert of Saint Macarius. Because there was no staretz in the Desert at that time, and therefore no possibility for starchestvo, about which the young novice had learned from the writings of Bishop Ignatius Brianchaninov, he went to Valaam. There he was able to enter into the practice of hesychasm.

The staretz, or elder, is a director of conscience and a novice master combined. He is selected by the hegumen from among the monks renowned for their wisdom, learning and mystical experience. The postulants, novices and professed monks are under his direc-

45

tion. They surrender their wills to him and do nothing without his permission. The staretz traces for them the whole programme of life they must follow. And every evening they come to him to confess their thoughts and deeds and to receive his instructions. The highest spiritual perfection is often reached by monks living under an experienced and saintly staretz. The Prayer of Jesus is commonly used to reach the heights of Christian perfection. This exercise consists in repeating devoutly, in appropriate conditions, this short prayer: 'Jesus Christ, Son of God, have mercy on me, a sinner.' This prayer, repeated with certain approved meditations, leads eventually to the recognition of one's own nothingness and to complete and joyful trust in Divine Providence. It is combined frequently with many other ascetic exercises. Instead of the Prayer of Jesus, which is inspired by the prayer addressed to our Lord by the blind Bartimaeus, any other short prayer may be used. The essence of the method consists in the realization of that constant Divine Presence which speedily leads to the practice of virtue and the contemplation of the highest truths. The Prayer of Jesus was introduced, or better reintroduced, into Russia by the disciples of Father Paissy Velichkovsky, a Russian himself, who lived in eighteenth-century Rumania. This practice is very old.

After a few years in Valaam, Father Isaya was transferred to the household of Archbishop Anthony of Tver, who, being a monk, held in greatest respect the monks of Valaam and periodically obtained trained novices for his monasteries from the Superior of Valaam. The hegumen selected Father Isaya and sent him to Tver, where he remained for a short time. Then, trained and experienced, he returned to Saint Macarius Monastery to be professed there.

Usually in the Orthodox Church the novitiate or probation lasts three years, though it may be prolonged. In Russia, an aspirant to the religious life visits a hegumen and requests permission to try his vocation. The hegumen, after deliberation, accepts the newcomer and hands him over to one of the elders to be initiated into the life. The probationer receives a robe and starts to grow a beard. He is called *poslushnik* — one learning to obey. Sometime after his three years of probation, the hegumen tonsures the novice, gives him a monastic name and gives him certain parts of the monastic habit, including the *mandorrhason* or *pallium*, a wide-sleeved cloak. He is now a *rhasophore*, bearer of the *rhason*. Henceforth he is incorporated into the monastic body and may not leave the monastery although he has not as yet made any vows. The next stage is profession. This is for life. It is usually made at the age of thirty for a man and forty for a woman. The *rhasophore* pronounces four vows: stability, obedience, poverty and chastity. He makes his profession by publicly giving affirmative replies to express questions of the hegumen. He does not recite or sign a formula as Westerners do. Then the rhasophore is tonsured and receives the little habit, including the *mandyas* and the *taramandyas*. The monk is now called *stavrophore*, because he wears a wooden cross. The ceremony of profession is very beautiful. Most of the monks, indeed an overwhelming majority, do not proceed to the highest stage in the monastic way, that which is called the stage of angelical perfection, the *skhimnik* or *megaloschemos*. No one is made *skhimnik* in Russia before passing thirty years as a stavrophore and being renowned for his piety. The *skhimnik* is usually professed by a bishop in a most beautiful and touching ceremony. He receives a special habit, which includes the *koukkoulion*, a veiled head covering, and the *analabos*, or embroided scapular. Fully dressed, the *skhimnik* looks quite similar to the Benedictine monk, except that his scapular is embroidered with the instruments of the Passion of Christ. Severe fasts and long prayers are prescribed for the *skhimnik*, who usually becomes a solitary or a recluse and sometimes a staretz.

Father Isaya lived peacefully in his monastery and even the fall of the Russian Empire did not disturb him much. Bolshevism changed things very little during the first years. To conform to the new law forbidding the ownership of land by ecclesiastical persons, the monastery was registered as an agricultural commune owned by the novices and employing the monks as hired laborers. Meanwhile the torrent of the Revolution rushed onward with full speed in the great world outside the monastery. On October 28, 1917, the Patriarchate of Moscow, suppressed by Peter the Great in 1720, was restored, and Metropolitan Tikhon of Moscow was elected in the old Kremlin as the Patriarch of all Russia to rule over one hundred and ten million Orthodox. He was an anti-Bolshevik and condemned the Communists and their teaching in his very first encyclical. The Bolsheviks, too weak as yet to molest the Church, left it in comparative peace until the Civil War was over. Then, in 1922, they started their first anti-religious drive using as an excuse that the clergy were unwilling to submit to the spoliation of churches. The great famine that broke out in Russia as a result of Communism furnished the Bolsheviks with the pretext to confiscate the Church's treasures, including sacred vessels, in order to sell them abroad in exchange for food for the starving provinces. The Patriarch agreed to deliver these vessels but in an orderly way and with a guarantee that the proceeds would be used properly. The Bolsheviks rejected his offer and imprisoned the bishops and laymen who resisted them. Many of the clergy were executed shortly afterward, including the saintly Benjamin Kazanski, Metropolitan of Petrograd. The Roman Catholic clergy also resisted. Archbishop Cipelae was arrested and Monsignor Budkevich executed. Patriarch Tikhon himself was subsequently imprisoned. His imprisonment led to many difficulties for the Russian Church. In the end there was a wholesale persecution of Christians of all denominations. When the Patriarch and most of the diocesan bishops were arrested, some priests sought to ingratiate themselves with the Soviets. They themselves became strongly imbued with Bolshevism. With the support of a Bishop Antonin Granovski, they proclaimed the Patriarch deposed and formed a temporary administration for the Russian Church presided over by Bishop Antonin. Later this group of Renovators became known as the Living Church.

The schismatic society was really quite moderate in its views, judging by the then existing standards. They proclaimed their conviction that the Soviet regime had come to stay for several decades if not for centuries and therefore the Church should try to conform to its demands. They also expressed their belief in the urgent need to modernize the canons and rites of the Russian Church to make it more comprehensible to the younger generation. They did not wish to change the dogmas. The Patriarch and his successors were constrained in due course to realize many aims of the Living Church, except for its more extreme innovations, such as the married episcopacy, marriage after ordination and new services.

The chief and unpardonable sin of the Living Church was rebellion against the Patriarch, which broke the unity of the Russian Church for several years and thereby enabled the Bolsheviks to develop their enormous godless propaganda. Gradually they reduced to utter impotence not only all groups within the Russian Church but also the Roman Catholics and Protestants, who were too weak to defend themselves.

At the beginning of the Soviet Revolution, Father Isaya, who was always of an ardent nature, entered into the struggle with the Renovators. As a result of his activities, he was arrested, imprisoned and sentenced to deportation to Siberia. He managed, however, to escape, crossed the Estonian border and was received into the monastic community of Pskovo-Petchersky. After a time there, he was ordained to the diaconate.

Father Isaya was a great admirer of Bishop Ignatius Brianchaninov, whom he preferred to that other great Russian contemplative, Bishop Theophan the Recluse. He knew the *Philokalia*, the *Sayings of the Desert Fathers* and the lives of many saints, especially Russians, by heart. The Holy Scriptures and the Fathers were always on his lips. Father Isaya was my first guide in the practice of the Jesus Prayer.

One wonderful June morning in 1926 I was sitting with him on a bench in the monastery garden. The blue dome of heaven was cloudless. Many birds were singing in the trees. The air was pure and perfumed with the fragrance of the blossoming flowers. The ancient churches of the monastery, with their small bulbous domes and shining gilded crosses were visible through the thick greenery of the flowering bird-cherries.

"Tell me, Father Isaya, how Bishop Ignatius understood the Prayer of Jesus. He was a very cultured man."

"Yes, he was indeed. According to Bishop Ignatius, the practice of the Prayer of Jesus is the bounden duty of all Orthodox, which they must not neglect. However, the external prayer alone is not enough, as Saint Seraphim of Sarov always insisted. God listens to our mind. Therefore, those who do not unite the external prayer with the inner one are not truly praying."

"Tell me, Father, how one starts to practice the Prayer of Jesus."

"In order to begin the practice of the Prayer of Jesus, the Bishop teaches us we must first lead a wise and abstemious life, avoiding all luxuries and all carnal pleasures. We must watch over our sight, hearing and other senses and limit our speech to the needful. This does not mean, however, that we should all retire into solitude. He who truly learns the Prayer of Jesus learns well how to live in true solitude. Several Fathers, like Alexis, the Man of God, Saint John the Tent-liver and Saint Vitalius practiced the ascesis of solitude of the heart and a true seclusion while still living in the world."

"Then what do we have to do?"

"We must first master our passions. This is done by frequent vocal prayer and psalmody. Then we may dare to practice mental prayer. Otherwise we may easily fall into spiritual illusion and diabolic temptations, have visions, hear voices, and so on. When we practice the Prayer of Jesus and any other kind of prayer, we should seek to acquire that special form of humility called *plach,* or lamentation. This is the sentiment of deep repentance, of salutary sorrow for committed sins and for our multifarious human weaknesses. This lamentation, or tears, is the only sacrifice that God accepts from fallen humanity before our soul is fully restored by the Holy Ghost through transfiguration. The penitential lamentation destroys passions, as fire burns dead wood, and introduces into our soul joy and serenity.

"Bishop Ignatius teaches us that prayer without penance, neglectful and self-interested, always leads to spiritual illusions, especially in the case of those who are inclined to daydreaming and have powerful imaginations. Progress in prayer is difficult. When you practice the Prayer of Jesus yourself, you will find that this is so. The prayer of attention demands self-sacrifice. They are few in number who are ready for this. We must have a true sorrow for our sins.

"And take note of this, my friend. The general sign of all spiritual states is deep humility, humble wisdom, setting our neighbor's good before our own, evangelical love of our neighbor, desiring to be unknown, and to leave behind worldly vanity. He who attains to true prayer experiences indescribable poverty of spirit when he stands up before the Lord God in prayer and presents to Him his requests."

"This is true, Father Isaya. I have always realized that those who practice true prayer do want to go apart, to be unknown, to leave behind all worldly vanity."

"We must pray, dear Brother Sergius, with great attention because when our mind is attentive then our heart responds with tenderness. Only then is prayer the common expression of both mind and heart together. The words of prayer should be said slowly in order that our mind can understand them and enter into the words of prayer. You can read all this in the writings of Bishop Ignatius."

"This is true for prayer in general, Father Isaya. What can you say of the Prayer of Jesus?"

"The same. The Prayer of Jesus is usually said thus: 'Lord Jesus Christ, Son of God, have mercy on me, a sinner.' We must say it first vocally. Then the vocal prayer will transform itself into mental prayer in due time. We should pronounce the Prayer in a low tone to be heard by none but ourselves. When we are overpowered by distractions, boredom, sadness or the like, then we should pronounce our Prayer loudly if we are alone in our cell. Vocal prayer awakens our soul from its heavy sleep caused by sorrow and boredom. When we experience an invasion of all kinds of thoughts and carnal de-

51

sires, the best thing to do is to pray loudly. Slow and deep breathing while we pray helps to keep our attention concentrated."

"When should I do this?"

"Now, when you start to pray in your cell. Make your own private rule how many bows and prostrations you should make. Those bows, when your head is brought to the level of your belt, as well as the great metanias or prostrations should be done slowly with sentiments of repentance. Say the Prayer of Jesus with each bow, standing in one place, keeping yourself recollected. Start with twelve bows. Do not increase their number vainly. We must do everything gradually."

"I heard, Father Isaya, of the Prayer of the Heart. What is that?"

"Do not try to find it, but practice solely penitential prayer. In due course you will find the place of the heart. When you feel within you poverty of spirit, tenderness of heart and tears, you may take it for granted that you are making progress in the right way. It is certainly good to have as a guide a staretz who has experience in the practice of the Prayer of Jesus and who is able to give you good advice."

Such was my first interview with Father Isaya.

Our second meeting took place a few days later in the upper garden of the monastery, from which one could see a vast panorama of fields and woods extending eastward into the Soviet Union.

"What do you think, Father, of the present state of the Russian Church? Can it survive the present trial?"

"It will certainly survive, my friend. The Russian Church has several wise and young bishops, like Bishop Alexis Simansky, auxiliary of Novgorod, whom I often met when I was caring for the affairs of the Desert of Saint Macarius and Bishop Nicholas Garushevich of Peterhof with whom I shared the struggles with the Renovators."

"And the Renovators, Father Isaya; will they remain or disappear?"

"They will disappear. Now in Russia there is a crisis of faith and the triumph of atheists. We can fight the crisis only with prayer and sacrificial living. The Renovators believed that they would establish themselves by flattering the government and with crafty speeches and vain talk before the believers. The latter see that the Renovators are opportunists who look for power and a comfortable living. They are indulgent toward human desires and passions because they are mastered by them. They consecrate married priests as bishops and allow second marriages to the secular clergy. They abolished monastic vows, pretending that they are against nature. The Renovators lack humility, prayer and simplicity.

"They look for an easier life on this earth. It is not the way of Christ, the way of the Cross."

"Can we continue our last talk, Father Isaya?"

"Why not? Bishop Ignatius distinguishes two stages in the practice of the Prayer of Jesus, which leads us to impassability. During the first stage we pray with effort, continually rejecting distracting thoughts and the attacks of passion. This is the time of labor. The second stage starts when we feel the presence of Divine Grace. The mind is now united with the heart. This is the Prayer of the Heart. Prayer becomes free of distractions and is accompanied with tender, penitential tears. Sinful thoughts lose their mastery over the mind, and life runs on serenely.

"At this time we should develop in ourselves humility and obedience to our spiritual father. The latter frees us from all cares. He who acquires true humility cannot be mastered by transitory things. He is freed from all sorrow and the burden of cares which can distract our minds and make our prayer fruitless. Only a very few attain solitude of mind, but we should not be depressed. Let us pray continually and patiently and the Lord will grant us in due course the pure Prayer of Grace. He who prays persistently with his impure prayer, never falling into depression when he sees no results, will attain in time pure, undistracted prayer.

"Bishop Ignatius states that the first fruits of prayer are attention and sweetness. The latter is born of the first. The sweet feeling of tenderness steadies the attention. Influencing each other, attention and tenderness make prayer deep and pure, suppress distractions and daydreaming, and make our hearts lively. Attention and sweetness, like true prayer, are gifts of God. By forcing ourselves to pray, we show our desire to acquire prayer. Our efforts to attain to attention and to tenderness demonstrate our will to gain them. The next fruit of prayer is an ever-increasing capacity to see our sins and our sinfulness. This increases our delicacy of feeling and leads to tears. Lamentations are an overflowing tenderness of heart, united with the sorrow of a humble and penitential heart. These tears proceed from the depths of the heart and envelop the soul.

"When the man of prayer receives this gift of tears he is overshadowed by the Divine Presence, death is very present to him and he fears judgment and condemnation. As he continues to progress, the man of prayer is penetrated with a refined, holy and spiritual sense of the fear of God. This sensation cannot be likened to any other sensation of the carnal or even of the merely spiritual man. This is something new. This fear of God melts passions, while mind and heart are irresistibly attracted to uninterrupted prayer.

"In time the contemplative attains a state of tranquillity, humility and a love of God and neighbor without distinguishing the good and the bad. At the same time, the soul acquires the ability to endure the sorrows permitted by God to heal his vices and to help him overcome his sinfulness. The love of God and neighbor, born from the fear of God, is radically different from merely human love. It is altogether spiritual, holy, refined and humble. Bishop Ignatius advises us to keep in our cells large icons of the Savior and of the Mother of God. They help us to realize better the presence of God and to behave accordingly. He also said that once we begin our rule of prayer it is inadmissible to abandon it, especially for long periods. It is better not to begin the exercises of prayer than to begin and then give them up. Into the soul that abandons the blessed alliance with prayer, passions flow as an irresistible flood and overpower it. The invading passions receive special power over such a soul. They install themselves solidly in such a soul and can hardly be overcome afterward.

Unbelief, cruelty, hardness of heart penetrate the soul. Devils once expelled by prayer return, burning with vengeance for their exile and in a greater number. According to the Gospel the last state of such a man is worse than the first.

"It is for this reason that the fate of apostates is so terrible. They become toys of the devil, full of evil, blasphemy, cruelty, despair, boredom. I witnessed many such cases during my struggle with the Renovators and with militant godless men in the courts and in prison."

"Tell me, Father Isaya, since you know the teachings of Bishop Ignatius so well, how have you applied them in your own life?"

"I have tried, of course, especially when I lived in Valaam and in my Novgorodian monastery. Later on, when the revolution came and propagandists started to visit our monastery and to corrupt novices and even monks, I was forced to fight with them and to plunge into a sea of evil and hatred. They are infectious. While we are little able to do good, to practice humility, patience and meekness, it is easy to pay eye for eye, tooth for tooth. I believe it is better for a monk to remain in his cell and to converse with God than to move about in the world. The ancient Fathers rightly said that a monk who often leaves his cell even for the sake of business returns in a worse state, full of worldly impressions and passions. By necessity I used often to leave my Novgorodian monastery and I learned by experience the truth of the Fathers' warnings."

In the days that followed I often met with Father Isaya to speak of various problems connected with the practice of the Prayer of Jesus. I stayed three months in Pskovo-Petchersky Monastery. I always recall those months with gratitude. I arrived in the beginning of June, at the end of spring, when bird-cherries and lilacs were blooming. The days were warm and sunny, perfumed and still. I used to talk also with the hegumen, Bishop John Bulin, auxiliary of the Metropolitan of Estonia, as well as with other monks, and with the novices, especially Brother Sergei Mironovitch Paul.

I left the ancient monastery one marvelous autumn evening in the beginning of September 1926. Father Isaya and Brother Sergei accompanied me to the station. After taking leave of the hegumen, we climbed into a horse-drawn carriage. Father Isaya took the driver's place, while Brother Sergei sat with me. Father Isaya took the reins and the horses started to trot. We crossed ourselves according to custom. We went up the hill to the Holy Gates of the monastery. I looked back. Ancient churches, white, cream, and pink, stood out boldly against the bright green background. The gilded crosses on the domes shone in the sunset. We passed through the gates and the ancient Pskovo-Petchersky Monastery dropped out of my sight for thirty-four years. I only saw it again in July, 1960.

The train was already in the station. I said good-bye to Father Isaya and to Brother Sergei. I never saw them again. Brother Sergei died in the forties. Father Isaya went to the Holy Land shortly after my departure. He settled in Jericho. I corresponded with him occasionally till the Second World War broke out. During the hostilities he also died. But his holy words remain firmly in my memory, very much alive, bringing me untold good.

CHAPTER 10

Sergei Mironovitch Paul

I first met Sergei Mironovitch Paul at Tartu in Estonia, during the year 1924. He was the eldest son of M.A. Paul who was one of the preferred disciples of Archimandrite Anthony Khrapovitzky at the Ecclesiastic Academy of St. Petersburg. His father remained a layman and rapidly climbed the bureaucratic ladder of the civil service. He became Vice-Governor of Estonia, the first Estonian to occupy that important post at the time of the Russian Empire. He died, still young, at the threshold of a brilliant career.

Sergei Mironovitch, after completing his secondary education, entered the university, but soon, because of the First World War, entered Military School and became an officer. He fought in the First World War and then, during the Civil War, received a terrible injury: he lost his left eye and became deaf in the right ear. A bullet had gone through his head and Sergei had to submit to a complicated operation every three years. Nevertheless, this had not made him a rebellious or bitter man. He was always friendly and well balanced and he never judged anyone. Except for the late Archbishop of Canterbury, Doctor William Temple, I have never met a person of such distinction.

Upon his return home, Sergei Mironovitch received his university degree with the notation *maxima cum laude* and he prepared himself to occupy the rostrum of analytic chemistry. But then instead of pursuing his career as a scientist, he entered the Monastery of

Pskovo-Petchersky as a novice. There was something about him which closely resembled the Prince Myshkin of *The Idiot* of Dosto-evsky but he reminded me even more of Alyosha in *The Brothers Karamazov*. Like the latter, Sergei Mironovitch was never preoccupied with food, drink, or clothing and everything worked out for the best. He never thought of his career and his manner was always straightforward. He gave to others everything he possessed.

He spent three years at the Monastery of Pskovo-Petchersky without professing his vows. Like Alyosha Karamazov, he returned to the world upon the advice of his staretz, Father Vassian. "Sergei Mironovitch," Father Vassian told him one day, "return to the world. Men like you are more needed there than here. Teach by the example of your life. When the proper time comes, and with the will of God, you may return here."

After his departure from the monastery, Sergei Mironovitch lived for some time with my brother Constantine. Later Sergei was named director of the laboratory of experimental chemistry. According to what I was told, he died in the year 1940.

Sergei Mironovitch had learned the Jesus Prayer from Father Ambrose in a Serbian monastery in 1920. He rapidly made progress in this Prayer and attained inner silence, serenity and continual joy. I had several conversations with him at Tartu and at the Pskovo-Petchersky Monastery.

One day he came to see me in my cell. This was one of the oldest cells in the monastery, dating back to the sixteenth century and the time of Saint Cornelius. According to tradition, the Czars, Ivan the Terrible and Peter the Great, had occupied this cell when they stayed at the monastery. This same cell had also been occupied by Hieromonk Lazar, who was visited by Alexander I and also by Hieromonk Theodosius the Recluse, who was visited by Nicholas II. It communicates with the crypt-church and with the caves by underground tunnels.

"Tell me, Brother Sergei," I asked the novice, "how have you gotten accustomed to your new style of life?"

"Very well. Much better than in Serbia where the Russian intellectuals were numerous. I feel much better off without them."

"Why?"

"Because simple folk, as we are here, are more unified, while the intellectuals, after leaving one shore do not get off at the other, and are thus unhappy. They have abandoned the ancient faith of our ancestors, but they are not capable of absorbing vulgar atheism, the brutality of our age and decadent morality. They limp on both feet. Here, only the superior and the monk-deacon are well educated, the others are simple people, peasants.

"When I first arrived here, the confessor of the Community, Father Vassian, told me: 'Well, Sergei Mironovitch, you have come to our monastery. You have already stayed in a monastery in Serbia. You know the monastic life. Bishop Theophan the Recluse wrote wisely: "If someone comes to a monastery, he must choose solitude, the church and the cell for prayer and work." That's all. Stay in your cell. It will teach you everything necessary. If you get involved in conversations with the brothers you may hear something vulgar and not edifying. You might then leave the monastery and lose your faith on seeing men who, after years of monastic life, are still full of envy, jealousy, vanity, and so on. You already know the Jesus Prayer; practice it and ask counsel of Father Arkadi. He knows many things about this subject.' So I live in this manner avoiding conversations and chatter. I am considered because of this, by certain monks, as a proud and arrogant person."

"Tell me, Sergei Mironovitch, is the Jesus Prayer really valuable?"

"Very useful. However, one must practice it with great humility so as not to fall into spiritual self-deception and to think of oneself as someone important. Without humility, we are nothing. The more someone exalts himself, the more he will be humbled. The opposite is also true."

"Sergei Mironovitch, you have studied thoroughly Hinduism and Buddhism. There, things are not as they are here."

"Indeed. They are different. For the Hindus and the Buddhists, evil is ignorance, attachment to perishable things and to the world full of evil. Salvation, for them, is the annihilation of the personality, blown out like a candle or lost like a drop in the ocean. However, there are also some remarkable people among them. One day I heard the following story:

A great and powerful Maharajah had a Divan, in other words a first minister, his cousin, young, rich and cultivated. He was much envied. One day, the Divan gave a great banquet in his palace. One of the guests, a foreigner, approached the Divan and told him: "You are a happy man. You are noble, young, rich, in full health. You have a nice family and all the wealth of this earth." And the Divan replied: "Do you believe that the wealth of this earth can provide happiness? It is rather an obstacle to freedom of mind because it chains us to things ephemeral and fleeting." That same night, the Divan called upon his most faithful servant and in his presence he took off his royal clothes to put on the saffron robe of the *sanayassi*, the Hindu ascetic. He took a cane and disappeared forever into the Indian night.

"With the Hindus, the one who becomes *sanayassi* loses his caste and dies to this life. However, he wins because of this, great spiritual freedom. He is no longer chained by anything. You see that even the Hindus and the Buddhists are capable of the greatest sacrifices to achieve freedom of mind. But we have a much better way with the Holy Gospel: *You will know the Truth and the Truth will set you free.*"

"This means that you came to the monastery to find the truth?"

"The monastery, Sergei Nikolaevitch, is a spiritual school, as stated by Saint Benedict whom you admire so much. However, a monastery is not a formal school, like a seminary, but a school of spiritual experience."

"But do you find here what you are seeking?"

"The staretz knows that better than I do. I wish to stay here, but if the staretz should send me into the world, I would go as Alyosha Karamazov did with the blessing of Staretz Zosima. Do you know, Sergei Nikolaevitch, that you are closer to Alyosha than I am? There remains in me much of the Prince Myshkin. You stay here for three months. Observe, ask counsel of the Fathers Arkadi and Vassian. This will be of great help to you when you leave for the West to live among people of another culture and different faith. Always practice the Jesus Prayer. I am maintained uniquely by that Prayer.

"Do you know, Sergei Nikolaevitch, to what conclusion I came after the Civil War? That it is impossible to build anything good based on violence. Violence brings forth more violence and an infernal cycle commences. The logical end is mutual extermination. I believe that from a Christian point of view it is better to submit to violence than to become a slave of anger and to burn for vengeance.

"It is said that Abba Sisoes, when asked if it was permitted to kill a thief or a savage enemy who attacked you, replied: 'No. One must place oneself entirely in the hands of God. All the evil that happens is the result of our sins and we must endure it. Divine wisdom tells us that. Violence is not eternal and it corrupts the torturer much more than the victim. During the Civil War atrocities were committed by everybody. And what was the result? The Whites were defeated and the Reds started to destroy one another. And this is only the beginning. Purges will eventually occur. We ourselves must avoid that. God is love and we must worship him in spirit and in truth. The Jesus Prayer is that worship in mind and truth.'"

CHAPTER 11

Doctor Eugone Nikolaevitch Rozov

I met Doctor Rozov at the Pskovo-Petchersky Monastery in 1926. He was the district doctor and also treated the monks, for which he was given accommodation on the first floor of the bishop's residence. At the time Eugone Nikolaevitch was over fifty years old and a widower. His son, a quiet and intelligent boy, attended the high school at Petchersky. They lived very simply. Doctor Rozov came from a pious family. He finished seminary but did not become a priest. He became a doctor with high honors after his medical training at the Tomsky University in Siberia.

Eugone Nikolaevitch was not only pious and well educated in theological subjects but also a very spiritual person. He had great humility and in many ways he showed that he loved his neighbor. He tried never to refuse anyone anything. If someone asked him to visit a sick person a long distance away, he did so without reimbursement. If asked for advice, he would give it. If asked to make a house call, he would make it. And he never had need for anything.

I visited him one evening. The aroma of lilacs and jasmine in the bishop's garden poured in from the open window. The ancient monastery churches, pink, pale yellow and white, with blue onion domes dotted with stars, stood out distinctly from the green background of the gardens in the clear evening light. There was a deep and solemn silence. In his small room a lamp was burning before an old icon. Eugone Nikolaevitch sat in an easy chair, clothed in a white Russian shirt girded with a belt of the same color. With his greying beard he reminded one of a country priest as he might sit in his parish house.

"Tell me, Eugone Nikolaevitch, how do you manage to be always in a good mood and never concern yourself with money or with how to make both ends meet — for so I am told that is the way you live? How can you do that?"

"People will tell you many things, Sergei Nikolaevitch, but I will tell you only one thing: as it says in the Scriptures, one must first seek the Kingdom of God and his righteousness, then the rest shall be added unto you. As you know I am the son of an archpriest. I completed my seminary training. In my childhood and youth, together with my parents, I often visited the Trinity Lavra of St. Sergius and the Optino and Valaam Monasteries.

"I once heard this story from the guestmaster at Optino:

A very rich merchant came from Moscow to go into retreat. The melting of the snow and the impassable roads forced him to stay three days longer. His son was with him. Before leaving, he asked the guestmaster: "How much do I owe you, Father, for my son and myself?" "As much as you like," replied the guestmaster. "And what if I give nothing?" "That's your business." "Then, most likely, out of a hundred pilgrims, only one pays you?" "That happens, but the hundredth one usually pays for the other ninety-nine." "Well, my son," said the merchant, "pull out your wallet; both of us owe for one hundred pilgrims each." The merchant payed willingly and was pleased to do it. And the Lord blessed him because he had nourished two hundred poor brethren.

"My father, Archpriest Nicholas Rozov, who has passed away, used to say, 'Eugone, when you become a doctor and poor people come to consult you, do not force them to pay and even more, buy medicine for them. The Lord will not forget you. You will live happily, your soul will always be peaceful and your conscience will not bother you.' This is what I do and I live happily. He who can pay, I thank, and he who cannot, I do the work for God. It is said in the Gospel that he who serves others in little ways, will be served by God.

"You see here for yourself that someone brought us some jars of wonderful jam and I don't even know who. Everyone brings either money or things. Not only is there plenty for my son and myself but we even give things away to others. Remember what the Apostle Paul writes: 'And having food and raiment, let us therewith be content. But they that will be rich fall into temptation.' Remember what it says in the Gospel: 'You cannot serve God and mammon.' Some greedy Pharisees laughed. But he who laughs last, laughs best. Even you should seek only that which is needful and everything else will be given to you into the bargain."

"But how must I do that, Eugone Nikolaevitch?"

"It is apparent that you are still a man from the world. Remember once and for all, that the most important thing is to attain peace in your soul and once that is achieved, you will lack nothing. For it is said: 'Acquire spiritual peace and thousands around you will be saved.' And those thousands will bring you so much that you will not know where to put it. To worry about things is absolutely needless. Those who do not believe should indeed worry about such things. Their concern is how to obtain everything, even by stealing from another. They say: 'We live only once and therefore we must profit as much as possible from earthly pleasures.' Well, later they will receive their reward when they come to understand that everything passes, everything breaks, everything becomes wearisome and that all their efforts have been in vain and without a future in this passing world.

"You, Sergei Nikolaevitch, will be traveling soon to foreign places, first to Belgium and then to France, to the Catholics and later, perhaps, to the Protestants. Nothing happens without God's will, and that means you must go, because all that will fall into place of itself.

You are beginning something new and unheard of, some sort of communion with the Catholics. Many see this as something suspicious and they see you as a person who seeks profit for himself. But they are mistaken.

"I am an old doctor and I have seen many people. You are a simple and guileless person, not to be numbered with those who seek material gain and for that reason you will experience many sorrows, extreme poverty, lack of understanding and disdain from others. Do not despair but endure this willingly and live simply, modestly and humbly and in good time you will receive your reward, something that you cannot even imagine now. I am speaking of the results of your efforts. Then you will understand what it is to receive 'a hundredfold in this life.' But at first one needs to suffer in order to attain peace and detachment, just as I am attempting. So, do not attach yourself to anything that passes. Go your own way. Have you read the *Philokalia*?"

"Yes, Eugone Nikolaevitch, but to be honest, I understand very little of it."

"In good time, through experience, you will come to understand all of it, when you have reached my age. Much is written there about guarding one's thoughts and about the Jesus Prayer. This Prayer will help you a great deal."

"Those living in the world and being young as I am, can they also practice this Prayer?"

"Yes, they can. The pilgrim in *The Way of a Pilgrim* was of your age when he started to practice the Prayer; also another man, a merchant from Orlov, named Nemitov. He was a millionaire, subjected to the strongest temptations but nevertheless reached such heights in prayer that even Staretz Macarius of Optino was amazed. At the end of his life Nemitov forsook everything to apply himself to the life of prayer. I am drawn to do the same, but I must properly set my son on his feet first.

"In prayer, as in everything, use moderation. It is written that Abba Matoes said: 'I prefer a light and steady activity, to one that is very painful at the beginning but is soon broken off.' Everything will come with time, one must only try hard. When Staretz Ambrose was asked to recommend 'promotion' for one of the monks, he replied, 'With time, everything will be given: the mandya, the priesthood and so on. All that will be given by the appropriate authorities but the Kingdom of Heaven cannot be given by anyone. For that one must strive on one's own.' So try hard to master the Prayer of the Heart, for the Kingdom of God is within you and the violent take it by force."

Part III

Finland

During the summer of 1954 Serge Bolshakoff went to Finland. There he visited friends in the north and then two monasteries. The silence of the seemingly unending forests and beautiful lakes made a deep impression on him but still more the talks he had with his hostess in Nerko-Jarve and the spiritual fathers in Konevitsa and New Valaam.

Chapter 12

Madame Nina Nikolaevna

I was with Madame Nina Nikolaevna on the balcony of her summer residence at Nerko-Jarve, a domain that is lost in the immense forests which stretch from the Baltic Sea to the tundra of Lapland. The villa was isolated in a nearly impenetrable area of the forest, on the shores of a tranquil lake. The setting sun gilded the calm waters. I always admired this lake and the play of colors on its surface. In the morning, before sunrise, the lake was a dark blue and at sunrise it became golden red, violet and black. The blue sky was without a cloud. Some birds were singing in the forest and the perfume of the flowers from the garden and the freshness of the lake floated on the air. The husband and children of Madame Nina Nikolaevna were already asleep but we stayed on the balcony, admiring the changing colors on the lake. The white night of the far north reigned here in all its beauty.

"Here, Nina Nikolaevna, the silence is profound, like that of another planet or of this one three centuries ago when the population was small and there were no trains, automobiles or airplanes. But even then the lovers of silence went towards the north, to the shores of the Arctic Ocean, to Solovky."

"I can really rest only here, Sergei Nikolaevitch," replied my hostess. "Here there is no one, no town, no village, only the forests and the lakes. It is tiresome to live in a large modern city with its

69

unceasing noise, polluted atmosphere and great multitudes. Where there are people, there is always intrigue, envy, calumny and the like. When I was young all these vanities and the noise were pleasing to me. I took the exterior for the truth. My first marriage was very unhappy. My first husband was handsome and intelligent but superficial, without rules, faith or principles. When everything ended in tragedy, I returned to the faith. I then went to Valaam to ask the counsel of Father John.

"'Do you know, Servant of God,' said Father John, 'that you must not fall into despondency and think that your life is finished? You are young and everything may change many times. The Lord never sends hardships beyond our strength. Always remember this well.

"'There exists a legend to this effect. A monk was much tormented by the difficulties of his life and murmured against God by asking for a lighter cross. One night, during his sleep, he dreamed that he was in an immense cavern and all the walls were covered with crosses. The monk could see crosses made of gold, silver, iron, stone and wood. A voice said: "Your prayer has been granted. Choose any cross you want, according to your strength." The monk started to look for the smallest and lightest cross. At last he found a small wooden cross and asked: "May I take this little cross?" "But that is your own cross," answered the voice, "all the other crosses are much heavier."'

"Father John then added: 'Your cross appears to be heavy for you, Madam, but as staretz and confessor I often hear of such horrors and it seems to me that you will not anger the Lord. Pray often. Repeat from time to time the Jesus Prayer and abandon yourself to the will of God. The Lord God himself will show you the path to follow. Then return here and I will tell you what I can.'

"A few years passed. I was working in a modest job and was living a quiet life. One evening I was invited to a dance. Though I was in my thirties a gentleman who was a bit older than I was invited me to dance. I accepted. We later met a few times. I was told that this gentleman was unmarried, respected everywhere and one of the richest men in Scandinavia. He is now my husband. Two or three months after our meeting he asked me to become his wife.

"My parents were very happy: what a grand wedding they planned. But the experience of my first marriage had taught me to be prudent. I asked for time to think and my fiancé agreed. I then returned to see my staretz at Valaam and I told him everything. He reflected for a few minutes and then he told me: 'Servant of God, remember what I told you a few years ago, that everything would arrange itself and that God himself would indicate to you the path to follow. Well, he brings you now to a higher social position. However, you must always remember that hardships and sufferings will never disappear, they will only change in form. Instead of the little wooden cross of a humble life, poor and unremarkable, you will receive a golden cross which is much heavier to carry. However, it is also bearable if you practice great acts of generosity and charity. Undoubtedly you will be envied; people will try to separate you from your husband and his family. But if you remain indifferent to the wealth and honors, and they will come rapidly, and to the vanity of the world, you will be able to maintain inner peace, especially if you practice the Jesus Prayer as much as possible. And here is another recommendation: go each year for one month to a very secluded area and there practice the Jesus Prayer as well as you can. You will see how helpful such a practice is.'

"Well, I have now been married many years and every year we come here. At first my husband and children were not too happy about the time in the monastery but now they themselves wait impatiently for the moment to come here. It is a paradise. And I must tell you that the staretz was right. The cross of the millionaire is heavier to carry than that of the poor and it is much more dangerous. It is so easy to fall into pride or to become as cold as marble to the suffering of others.

"There is now, at New Valaam, a remarkable staretz, Hieroschimonk Michael the Recluse. Discuss with him your difficulties

71

in life and he will give you good advice. I have always observed in my life that if we persevere in our efforts to obtain something in spite of ever increasing obstacles, we manage, sometimes by superhuman effort, to gain the desired object but it is to our own loss and not for our good. We exert ourselves so much that we become indifferent to everything else or we realize that the result was not worth our efforts. What comes from God, comes by itself. The Scriptures say that the Kingdom of Heaven does not come in a noticeable way because the Kingdom of God is within us.

"A long time ago, when I was experiencing great sorrows with my first husband, I told my aunt, a very wise person, 'I will leave my husband and our house. Then I will be joyful and happy as I was before.' My aunt replied: 'I can see that you are still young. It is impossible to escape from yourself; but if you possess peace of soul, you would be happy and joyful anywhere. In this life it is impossible to escape from sorrows; it is necessary to have patience, to pray and wait. Then the Lord will show you the path at the moment that he chooses.' This is so true but young people cannot understand it."

We remained in silence. The lake had become wholly black.

"It is already eleven o'clock," observed Nina Nikolaevna, "but it is as light as day. It is time to rest, Sergei Nikolaevitch. Good night."

CHAPTER 13

Father Dorofey

Ⅰ arrived at Uusi Konevitsa one August evening in 1954. The setting sun illuminated the endless pine forests with a golden shine. I traveled on the horse-driven vehicle of the monastery. Suddenly the forest ended and I saw the meadows, the lake and, behind the latter, again forest; a typical Finnish landscape. We came to a wooden cottage which reminded me of those of northern Russia.

"This house will be your residence here," the driver told me, showing me into a large room with two windows and a big stove. In the eastern corner I saw a fine icon of Our Lady of Kazan with a red lamp burning before it. The room also contained a bed, a table and two chairs. When I was alone I found I liked my cell and the deep silence that surrounded everything. It was a true hermitage. I looked out of the window. The sun was just topping the trees of the forest and the lake was golden. On the shore of the lake I saw the old Russian bell-tower and the monastery.

Somebody knocked at the door and I heard the monastic prayer well known to me, "Lord Jesus Christ, Son of God, by the prayers of our holy Fathers, have mercy upon us." I answered, "Amen," and opened the door. Father Dorofey stood before me. "Father Hegumen is away today," he said, "and I came to welcome you, Sergei Nikolaevitch. I am the second Superior, Father Dorofey. Come with me to the monastery for supper."

"Do you know, Father Dorofey," I said, "that your monastery reminds me of the Kerzhenetz sketes on the Volga and the invisible monastery of Nestiar?" And I told this monk about my conversation with my mother in Petrograd in 1918.

"In the legend about Nestiar," Father Dorofey observed, "there is a large amount of truth. The startzy exist even now, even in the Soviet Union but they are unknown. They avoid publicity. For the contemplative, the retired life in a distant and obscure monastery, like this one, is the best. Did you notice that Russian monks through-out our history always avoided big towns and thickly populated prov-inces? They moved from southern Russia into the central provinces and then farther and farther to the north, even crossing the arctic circle to reach places like Petchenga Monastery here in Finland. They did so not merely to save themselves from Mongol raiders, but in search of silence and peace. It is said: 'In peace is His abode.' This is true."

After a simple supper I went to the chapel for compline. The chapel was very simple and small. I noticed some old icons, espe-cially the much venerated icon of Our Lady of Konevetz brought from Mount Athos to Russia in the fourteenth century by Arseny of Konevetz. The sanctuary lamps before the icons were lit. The golden rays of the setting sun illuminated the chapel. It was eight o'clock in the evening but it was still full daylight. In that latitude there is prac-tically no night in summer. The sun moves around the sky going slowly below the horizon for less than one hour of golden twilight and reappears again. The perfume of the blooming shrubs penetrated the chapel mixing with the warm air. There were about twelve monks or a few more in the stalls.

I remembered a similar service in Pskovo-Petchersky Monas-tery in 1926 and still earlier days at the sketes on the Kerzhenetz. Here the same silence and peace prevailed yet it seemed even deeper — the troubled world of the great cities of Europe and America was far away.

It touches a certain chord in my heart when I think of that small monastery lost in the vast forests of the North, in the stillness and amongst the giant conifers and the tranquil lakes. Konevitsa always reminded me of the Skete of Saint Nilus Maikov on the river Sorska in the dense forests of the Rostov country. The few small houses that made up the skete stood out on the slope of the hill by the lake. On the edge of the meadow there was a primitive clock tower. I myself lived in a log cabin at the edge of the forest. The skete had no church as such. A large room in one of the dwellings served the purpose. The community was small and most of the monks were getting on in years but they performed the services with fervor and piety. These monks had come from their original and large monastery of Konevetz, on the island of Konevetza, on the Lake of Ladoga, the largest lake in Europe. The island was occupied by the Red Army during the Second World War. The monks took away with them only the most necessary and holy things in their hasty evacuation. Their life now in Konevitsa was simple and very poor.

Father Dorofey was well over sixty when I first met him, but he looked young and strong. And he was full of joy. As the saying has it: "The soul united to God is always radiant." He came to Valaam at the beginning of the century as a very young man. Professed in Valaam, he was sent to Konevitsa later on. The community there had begun to diminish after the First World War, when it was cut off from its recruiting grounds in Russia. The Orthodox in Finland were too few to maintain two large monasteries.

It was with a certain eagerness that I consulted this wise old monk from Holy Russia who had lived through the painful transition period and could still smile radiantly. "Your Konevitsa, Father Dorofey, reminds me much of the Skete of Saint Nilus of Sora. The same solitude, the same silence, the same peace."

"Have you read, Brother Sergius, the *Tradition of Sketic Life* by Saint Nilus?"

"Yes, I have, Father. It was sent to me from Mount Athos a long time ago."

"That is good. You should read the *Tradition* frequently and meditate on it. Its contents cannot be understood at once but they reveal themselves gradually according to your spiritual growth. The sketic tradition is useful for all those who practice the Prayer of Jesus, especially its teaching on how to distinguish good thoughts from dangerous ones. If you fail in this, your progress in prayer will be slow, hardly possible."

"Could you summarize the teaching of Saint Nilus for me, Father? Because in the *Philokalia* and even in the *Tradition* there are many repetitions and many things that are not clear."

"Certainly. Saint Nilus did not write a textbook and what he wrote he wrote in the style of his age. Nevertheless, it is not difficult to summarize his teaching. The saint begins with *prilog*, that is, an idea or an image, which appears in our mind or heart. This thought might be suggested by the devil, who incites us to do one thing or another. This *prilog* might be sinless in itself; then it merits neither blame nor praise. We cannot avoid having thoughts passing continually through our minds, even undesirable ones. Only those who have attained to great holiness can do so, and even they can do it only for a time, as Saint Isaac the Syrian teaches us.

"The next stage, called *connection* by the Desert Fathers, is our *discussion* [interior dialogue] with the 'appearing thought.' This might be passionate or passionless. We make *connection* when we retain the suggestion of the devil, fall in with it and allow it to stay with us by our own choice. This the Fathers do not consider blameless but in the end it might work out for the glory of God. This comes about when the monk does not resist the sinful suggestion but discusses it within himself to the extent that the devil starts to make other suggestions. Then the monk comes to his senses and opposes the evil suggestion with a good one. For example, the devil suggests that I drink a glass of vodka. I accept this suggestion and come to the conclusion that in such bad weather to drink a glass of vodka would not only be pleasant but also very useful for my health to avoid the flu. But, immediately, I counter the suggestion with another thought. Although it would certainly be pleasant and perhaps healthful to drink a glass of vodka in this raw weather, I would be tempted to drink another glass, and a third, and gradually form a habit of drinking and become an alcoholic with all its accompanying misery. The evil suggestion leads me to think of the virtue of sobriety and I reject the evil proposal.

"The third stage is called by Saint Nilus *fusion*. This takes place when we accept the evil thought or image and enter into dialogue with it mentally and finally decide to do what the thought urges us to do. When an experienced monk who knows how to resist temptation and has been honored with divine assistance in the past, by neglect or laziness allows this fusion to take place, it is sinful. The case is different for novices and weak people. If they accept the suggestion but soon after repent and confess their sin before the Lord and invoke his assistance, God readily forgives them in his mercy. Their kind of *fusion* can be easily understood and forgiven. They were overpowered mentally by the devilish suggestion but in the depth of their hearts they preserved their attachment to God. Therefore, since sin was unrealized in the act, their union with him remained unbroken. The second kind of *fusion*, according to Saint Gregory of Sinai, is this: We accept devilish suggestions by our free will. We are overcome to such a degree that we cease to resist them and decide to satisfy our passion at the first opportunity. If we do not act at once it is only because we lack the opportunity. Such a state of soul is very sinful. This happens for example when a person decides to fornicate but remains physically chaste because he lacks the opportunity but he will fornicate once there is an opportunity.

"The next stage is *imprisonment*. Our heart is irresistibly attracted to the seducing thought. We retain it within us. We carry on a mental discussion with the idea which disturbs our whole spiritual life. This happens, for example, in the case of vengeance. *Imprisonment* also has two degrees: the first, when our mind is overpowered by some idea and our thoughts turn continually to the devilish suggestion. Still we are able with divine assistance to turn our mind from wandering about and call it back to its business. The second is when our mind is overwhelmed as by a tempest. We find it impossible to return to our former quiet and peace. This results from worldly distractions and too much idle talk. We see here how important it is to keep silence.

"Our sinfulness is measured by the way we are overpowered: whether this happens during prayer in church or in private, whether the obsessive idea is passionate or not, whether it is indifferent or truly sinful. When devilish temptations are entertained during prayer, when our minds should be turned to God and be free of outside thoughts, this is very sinful. But when worldly thoughts come upon us outside of prayer time, this is natural enough. If these thoughts are simple and permissible and our mind remains generally concentrated, everything is all right.

"For the fathers, passion is an inclination of the soul that is fostered so long that it becomes a habit, almost part of our nature. We arrive at this by our own free will and desire. The obsessive and sinful idea becomes rooted firmly within us because we continually mull over it, nourish and cultivate it in our heart. Thus it becomes a habit and continually disturbs us with its passionate suggestions coming from the devil. Our foe then unceasingly pictures before us some object or some person and urges us to an exclusive love. Against our will we are overpowered and become slaves to that thing or person. This leads to a neglect of prayer and a continuous preoccupation with the object. Thus a drunkard continually thinks of when and how he can obtain his drink, the fornicator is obsessed with women, the worrisome person with his money, and so on.

"Every passion must be purged away by a penance in this life equal to its gravity. Otherwise we must suffer for it in the world to come. Also, we must repent and pray or we will be punished for our lack of repentance. Those who have been overpowered by passion must struggle against it and avoid all occasions that could revive it. For example, those who are vengeful must avoid the places where their offenders reside, those who are tempted to unchastity must avoid the persons who excite them, and so forth. Those who neglect the necessary precautions, first of all kill their foes or seduce women in their imagination; then, in due course, they commit the crime in fact. The ancient fathers teach us that we must withstand passion boldly. Ultimately, we shall triumph or we shall be defeated in our mind. He who vanquishes the foe will receive the crown, while he who is defeated will endure eternal punishment. The best method to fight evil suggestions is to cut off the very first *prilog* and to practice unceasing prayer. You see, all this is quite simple," Father Dorofey finished with a big smile.

"Is all this confirmed by your experience, Father?"

"Certainly. I saw this myself in Valaam. In the old days quite a few drunkards were sent from St. Petersburg to Valaam to be healed. They were habitual drunkards, mostly from wealthy business families. They usually remained in Valaam for three years. Valaam was an island and its only inhabitants were monks. There were no taverns, nowhere to find vodka. Drunkards were usually employed as laborers and expected to do hard work. Church services, work and talks with the spiritual father, that was the programme. A good many were completely cured within the three years, becoming teetotalers. Vodka became repulsive to them. The same thing happened to fornicators."

A few days after my arrival I had a long talk with Father Dorofey. "It seems to me, Father," I said, "that your small monastery is a very good place to practice the Jesus Prayer on account of its isolation and silence."

"You are right, Sergei Nikolaevitch. Those who want to progress in this prayer should live in places where silence and solitude are reigning. One can practice this prayer anywhere but those who want to attain prayer of the heart should live accordingly. Both of the great Russian writers of the last century, Bishops Ignatius Brianchaninov and Theophan the Recluse, left their sees in order to practice that prayer freely. Do you practice the Jesus Prayer yourself?"

"Yes, I try."

"Well in that case you know something. Repeat the prayer, as often as you can, vocally or mentally, according to circumstances, without hurrying — rather plaintively as penitent and sinner, asking for pardon. Do it regularly and try to live, as much as you can, according to the demands of the Gospel. If you do this for a long period you will find great peace of soul. Neither the hardships of life nor humiliations imposed upon you by others will trouble you. This is wonderful. Saint Seraphim of Sarov said to Timon, Abbot of Nadeev: 'Attain peace of soul and thousands of people will be saved around you.' Prayer, of course, is essential but also an ascetic life, even if you live in the world. Patience and humility are necessary. Without them we cannot progress in prayer. We all love humility but in others, not in ourselves. We like to judge other people but hate it when we ourselves are reprimanded. Yet for our own salvation it is of paramount importance.

"When we are reprimanded and criticized we discover our faults and the weaknesses of which we had not even an idea. For this reason it is better to begin the exercise of the Jesus Prayer in the world, among people. Those who want at once to lead a solitary life, as hermits or recluses, are ignorant of most of their faults. And we must be always watchful, especially those who live in the world amidst all its temptations. The continuous repetition of the Jesus Prayer is the continuous remembrance of God. We learn how to walk before God. First, we practice vocal prayer, then mental, then prayer of the heart, without words and images. It is walking in the presence of God, a sense of his presence and of his providence. Not many reach this stage but some do by the grace of God. I have met such people in my life. And one thing more. Never reveal your own experience to others, except to your staretz. Otherwise you can easily lose everything you gained."

A few days later, Father Dorofey visited me in my log cabin. The sun was setting. Its golden rays shone on the giant trees and on the tranquil lake. The profound silence of the Far North reigned supreme. The red sanctuary lamp flickered before the icon in the corner honoring a Presence. I was reading the *Tradition of Sketic Life* of Saint Nilus of Sora.

"Are you reading Saint Nilus of Sora?" asked Father Dorofey. "Read him with care and try to apply his words to your own life."

"Well, Father Dorofey, I read here that any idea coming to us in prayer time, even a good one, should be rejected at once, because it distracts us from our prayer. On the other hand, if a thought comes to us outside the time of prayer, we must cut it off at once if it is sinful. Other thoughts should be admitted only after due consideration because bad thoughts often accompany a good idea. Is that not so?"

"Exactly. We must examine the thoughts coming to us. If an idea comes to us and appears to be a good one yet we feel some uncertainty and hesitation about it, we must reject such a thought and look into the depths of our heart and say: 'Lord Jesus Christ, Son of God, have mercy on me, a sinner.' This prayer can be varied. We may say the first half at one time, 'Lord Jesus Christ, have mercy.' This prayer should be said slowly, standing, sitting or lying down. We must enclose our mind in our heart and breathe slowly; deep, slow breathing is very useful for the concentration of our mind during prayer. Experience will quickly teach you that."

"But, Father Dorofey, if my attention is still distracted, what should I do?"

"When we cannot pray in the solitude of the heart, that is, without outside thoughts, and when the latter grow and multiply, we must not lose courage but persevere in our prayer. Saint Gregory of Sinai said that no beginner is able to keep his attention concentrated and free of alien thoughts without extraordinary help from God. Only very spiritual and experienced persons are able to remain attentive and withstand the invasion of thoughts and then not by their own strength but by God's grace.

"Therefore, my brother in Christ, when alien thoughts, especially impure suggestions come to you, take no notice of them but, reducing your breathing and shutting up your mind in your heart, continue to call on the Lord Jesus. If even then attention cannot be attained, we must pray to be saved from those very thoughts. If even this is of no avail, we must pray out loud, pronouncing the words slowly, patiently and firmly. If we feel ourselves weakening or in despair, we must still call on God, asking for his help and never giving up prayer. If we are firm, temptation will vanish. Experience teaches us this. When our serenity is restored and we free ourselves from the overpowering and obsessing idea, we must again go back to silent prayers. Solitude is the exclusion during prayer of all alien thoughts, even those that seem good to us. To keep the mind in the heart, excluding all foreign ideas while praying, is hard work until we form the habit and experience the sweetness of prayer in the heart by the action of Divine Grace. Many people give up prayer because of their weakness and impatience, expecting quick results. Those who are overshadowed by grace pray easily and with love. Their prayer is sweet and free from captivating ideas."

"What can you say, Father Dorofey, about the hesychast method of prayer?"

"You mean, my friend, the prayer described in the *Philokalia*? This method is of secondary importance. We can learn how to pray well without this method. It is true, of course, that deep and rhythmic breathing helps to concentrate our attention. But it is merely a method. People are advised to sit on a low chair, inclining their head and neck, concentrating their mind in their heart and then say the Prayer. It means simply that we must pray attentively and with feeling. When our mind becomes tired from the effort of this exercise and the heart feels pain on account of the unceasing calling on Christ, we start singing psalms in order to have a change. Yet if prayer is sweet we should not leave it to sing psalms. In order to avoid spiritual illusions while praying, we should not entertain any pictorial representations in our mind, though they will come even when our mind remains in our heart. Only those illuminated by the Holy Spirit are able to keep their mind unmoved, free from all thoughts and images. True unceasing prayer is a state in which we persevere at all times in the adoration of God. This adoration is free from words and images."

"When we are praying, must we reject not only visions and voices but also abstract philosophical speculations?" I asked Father Dorofey.

"Yes. Saint Nilus believed that those who do not practice the Prayer of Jesus, which is the source of many virtues and of spiritual joy, should sing and read psalms in the services, often and at length. However, those who have progressed well and are filled with the Grace of the Holy Spirit do not need long services but, rather, the silence of unceasing prayer and contemplation. Of course, this is more suitable for hermits than for those living in communities. Solitaries, when they are united to the Lord in the Prayer, must not leave their conversation with him and be confused by vocal prayer."

"What do you think, Father Dorofey, of this quotation from Isaac the Syrian which I have copied:

Those who have experienced this spiritual and desirable joy know that this suddenly puts a stop to vocal prayer because the lips, the tongue, the heart, treasurer of thoughts, and the mind, guide of feelings and thought, cease to act. Then the mind has no more prayer but is moved on by another force not its own. The mind is mysteriously captured and experiences something indescribable. This state is called "ecstasy" or the "vision of prayer." This is no longer prayer, properly speaking, because the mind is above prayer and has no desire. The soul of the ascetic now enters into an incomprehensible union, becoming truly God-like. It is illumined in all its movements by the ray of Eternal Light. The mind begins to experience something of future beatitude. It forgets itself and everything transitory, everything earthly. There is no more prayer, no matter how pure. The soul is filled with indescribable joy, the heart overflowing with transcendent

sweetness, which penetrates the very body. We then forget all merely human passions and even life itself and are
certain that the Kingdom of Heaven is nothing more than
the state in which we are.

"What do you say of this?"

"My dear Brother Sergius, of such things they alone can speak
who have experienced them personally. If you have had such experience in any degree, you should consult Father Michael at New
Valamo. He has been both a hermit and a recluse and has had much
experience. Personally, I may only repeat the words spoken by Saint
Poemen the Great to a pilgrim who asked him about many things,
spiritual and transcendent. At first, Abba Poemen answered not a
word. When he was asked why he remained silent, he replied, 'If I
were asked about passions and sins and how to heal them I would
reply with joy but this pilgrim asks me about spiritual things which
are unknown to me.' When the visitor asked Saint Poemen how to
fight passions and to avoid sins, the Egyptian ascetic became happy
and said: 'Now I shall open my mouth.'"

I had many talks with Father Dorofey during my stay in the
little log cabin at the edge of the forest. One day I asked Father: "How
does one reach spiritual peace?"

"One needs *ougomonitsya*," replied Father Dorofey smiling.

"What is meant by *ougomonitsya*?"

"Well, here it is! When I was a young novice at Valaam the
staretz whom I served, once told me: 'Dimitry, it will be hard for you
to achieve *ougomonitsya*. You have such a cheerful and active dis-
position. But if you do not quieten, you will not attain pure prayer
and your monastic life will be futile. What good is it to be a monk if
you are not a man of prayer?' Then I asked him, as you asked me
today, 'What is meant by *ougomonitsya*?' The staretz told me, 'It is
very simple. Now it is summer and you most likely are waiting for
autumn when there will be less work in the fields.' 'That's true, Father,' I replied. 'Well, autumn will come and you will be looking for-

84

ward to winter, the first trek through the snow and the holy days. And when they arrive you will be waiting for Pascha, the bright feast of Christ's Resurrection? Isn't that so?' 'That's true, Father.' 'Now you are a novice, but most likely you are waiting for the time when you will become a rassophore monk?' 'Yes, Father.' 'And then you will be waiting for the small schema and then for the priesthood. All of this means that you have not achieved inner stillness, do not have *ougomonitsya*. But when everything is all the same to you, spring or autumn, summer or winter, Christmas or Pascha, novice or schema-monk, and you live for the day, for "sufficient unto the day is the evil thereof," and you are not dreaming and waiting but have surrendered yourself totally to the will of God, then you will have achieved *ougomonitsya*.'

"Many years passed after this conversation. I received the mantle and the priesthood and yet I waited for something. My job was changed to that of head cook. I did not want this but I had to obey. Well, when they finally sent us out here during the last war, I came gladly while others wept because of the loss of our fine monastery on Lake Ladoga, which is occupied now by the atheists. Everything is God's will. If you accept God's will calmly and with love and do not expect your own fancies to be fulfilled, you will have *ougomonitsya*. Yet you are far from this, Sergei Nikolaevitch. You are still seeking your own will. But without achieving *ougomonitsya* it is impossible to attain pure prayer!"

"Tell me, Father Dorofey, what is pure prayer?"

"It is prayer without idle thoughts, when the mind does not wander, the attention is not distracted and your heart is awake, that is, feels fear and compunction. When you pray only with your lips and your thoughts are far away, that is not prayer."

"And how does one acquire pure prayer?"

"Through hard work, of course. Have you heard of the Jesus Prayer?"

"Yes, I have."

"Have you tried to practice it?"

"I have tried."

"And did it go well?"

"Poorly."

"Do not despair. Repeat it over and over to yourself and it will come in its own good time."

"How does one know that one has attained pure prayer?"

Father Dorofey looked at me searchingly and asked: "Have you heard of Staretz John of Moldavia?"

"No."

"The monk Parfeny Aggeev writes of him in his *Travels*. Have you ever read this book?"

"No."

"Read it. It is very instructive and useful. Once Parfeny asked him about pure prayer. Staretz John answered that when he began to practice the Jesus Prayer he had to force himself a great deal but then it became easier and easier. Finally the prayer caught on and began to flow like a stream in him. It began to move by itself; it murmured and gurgled and touched his heart. Well, Father John began to isolate himself from people; he went to a small hermitage. He ceased to accept visits not only from laywomen but also from laymen and only rarely from monks. Then there came to him an irresistible urge to pray. Parfeny asked the staretz, 'What is this irresistible prayer?' Father John replied: 'This is irresistible prayer: I stand up to pray in the evening before sunset and when I come to myself the sun is already high in the sky and I have not even noticed it.' That is pure prayer."

"Tell me, Father Dorofey, how necessary is pure prayer for those in active life, for example, missionary work?"

"It is very useful. When a person undertakes to practice the Jesus Prayer then he becomes, let us say, like a lime-tree in bloom. When there are no blossoms on the lime-tree, then the bees do not come. But when this tree begins to bloom, then the aroma of its flowers attracts bees from everywhere. So it is with an ascetic who has become firmly established in the Jesus Prayer. The aroma of this prayer, the virtues which it produces, attract from everywhere good people who are seeking to learn real prayer. He who lives in Christ, God carries him as a child in his own hands. He need not worry about anything. From all quarters good people throng to him and protect him as the apple of their eye. He who practices the Jesus Prayer finds peace under the shadow of the Lord. And he has no cares. Everything comes automatically."

"Do sorrows also come for such a one?"

"Of course they come, but they, too, are turned into joy. However, you are unable to understand this secret yet. It is beyond you. But it will come in good time."

"Tell me, Father Dorofey, can one be saved in the world?"

"And why is it impossible? The Kingdom of God is within us when we prostrate ourselves deeply in our hearts before the Lord and offer to him the sweet smelling incense of pure prayer. Have you read *The Way of a Pilgrim?*"

"Yes, I have."

"Well, you can act accordingly. Nemitov, a rich merchant from Orlov, was a layman, but amazed the Optino Staretz Macarius with the depth of his prayer. Yet even Nemitov when he reached the highest degree of prayer became a recluse and retired to his own house. For one who has begun to live with God and has seen the greatness of the spiritual world, it is difficult to remain in the world. Just like an eagle, he soars on the heights, and unlike a hen, he cannot take pleasure in bustling along the roadside."

We were sitting on a bench on the shore of a quiet lake. White feathery clouds sailed across the blue sky and the sun was setting. The trunks of the tall fir trees shone like bright candles in the setting rays. The lake, all gold, was like glass, framed by the green of the woods. The silence of the far north reigned everywhere.

"And so, my friend," Father Dorofey pointed out, "when your heart becomes like this evening, just as quiet and peaceful, then the light of the unsetting sun will shine upon it and you will understand through experience what pure prayer is."

"Tell me, Father Dorofey," I asked him after some time had lapsed in silence, "how can we find out God's will for us?"

"The Holy Fathers tell us that life's circumstances show us this. With faith we can also ask a staretz or another wise person what we should do. We can also judge the inclinations of our heart. Then pray three times for the Lord to show us his will, just as the Savior prayed in the garden of Gethsemane. And where the heart inclines, go that way.

"We should live in the present. The past can teach us how to avoid sin and thus become part of the present. The future is unknown to us. The one who lives a saintly life prepares a saintly future for himself. When a person attains peace of mind he is always in good humor because he experiences the continuous Providence of God in his life."

On the day of my departure from Uusi Konevitsa I said to Father Dorofey: "Yes, your little monastery is a true Nestiar. I met some very spiritual monks here, true startzy. And yet the world outside knows nothing of you." Father Dorofey smiled and said to me, "This is all to the good. Having a great many visitors destroys a contemplative community. Here we are a few and old. Within a few years the survivors will go to Uusi Valamo to join that community and Uusi Konevitsa will cease to exist. But don't be dismayed. There are other similar communities in the world. You will learn of them in due course. Above all, try to attain peace of soul for yourself, then you will not need external help."

CHAPTER 14

Father John

When I think of Father John there comes to my mind that wonderful summer evening in New Konevitsa, in Finland. The rays of the sun shine in upon the altar. Father John stands before it, presiding at the Vesper Service. His golden phelonion is like a living flame. And his face, too, shines as though illumined from within. I stand in a corner of the sanctuary. From the open window I see the cloudless blue sky, the still, broad lake and the endless forests. The service progresses slowly. The monks sing unhurriedly. Everywhere there is peace, an atmosphere of deep, pervading silence. The Holy Mother of God looks down upon us from the ancient icon of Our Lady of Konevetz, brought by Saint Arseny from Mount Athos in 1393.

Father John had been ordained a priest only a short time before we met. He had begun his monastic life in the monastery of Saint Arthemy of Vervholsk, one of the most attractive monasteries of the Far North, on the river Pinega, four hundred kilometers from Arkhangelsk, on the White Sea.

This monastery is surrounded by impenetrable forests, tundras and marshlands. Roads and even footpaths are rare. It is true solitude. Anyone who visits Vervholsk Monastery is greatly impressed by its surroundings. Without any difficulty the visitor forgets the world of teeming cities, vanities of all sorts and much unhappiness. His soul is immersed in a quiet yet luminous contemplation of a nature perpetually wrapped in winter and its solemn stillness. The vanity of a worldly life, the unavoidable reality of death, readily come to mind. And yet these thoughts cause no depression but rather a peculiar joy, one that is quiet and a little sad. The visitor, far removed from all earthly distractions and temptations, cannot but think of his interior life and of its need to be reinvigorated. According to the monastic saying, "Church and cell will teach you how to live and what to do."

Some time after his tonsure, Father John was invited to the Saint Trifon Monastery at Petchenga on the Russo-Norwegian border, far beyond the Arctic Circle. Surprisingly, because of the nearness of the Atlantic Ocean and the warm current of the Gulf Stream, the climate of Petchenga is mild for such a high latitude. The average winter temperature is only six degrees below zero Celsius and frosts fifteen degrees below are very rare. Spring begins at the end of April at Petchenga after a month of rain and fog. Numberless migratory birds come to the tundras and the fishing season begins. In May the rivers become free of ice. The summer season begins in July and lasts two months. The average temperature is only eight degrees Celsius but it may rise to twenty-two degrees. The weather is warm and still. Nowhere in the world does the forest come so far north as at Petchenga. These arctic forests are silent. There are many birds but they do not sing. And there are many flowers. The long, warm, silent days of summer have their own special charm. The sun shines all twenty-four hours and the blue sky is cloudless. Because of the purity of the air the distant mountains are clearly and sharply visible.

Autumn, like spring, is rainy and foggy. Winter returns early in November, and on December ninth the sun disappears to show itself again only on February fourth. Nevertheless, the polar night is not a continuous darkness, an unrelieved gloom. The white snow gives some relief. And when the aurora borealis begins to play, which it does frequently, it is bright enough to read with ease. There are, too, wonderful starry displays and floods of moonlight. At the beginning and at the end of the long night there are sunrises and sunsets that color the horizon for hours even though the sun does not appear. On the whole the climate of Petchenga is healthy and the local inhabitants have a reputation for longevity.

In my childhood I knew people who visited the Skete of Saint Nicholas, the northernmost monastery of the Russian Empire, situated near the settlement of Malyye Karmakuly on the island of Novaya Zemlya in the Arctic Ocean. Novaya Zemlya reminds one of New Zealand in the Pacific Ocean. It is about the same size and is really two islands separated by narrow straits. Novaya Zemlya is about fifteen hundred kilometers long and four hundred kilometers wide. Its terrain and climate are exceedingly rugged. The island itself is a conglomeration of rocks and stones. Snow lies in the mountains nearly all year round. And there are ice-fields. The arctic night in Novaya is longer than in Petchenga. The average winter temperature is twelve degrees below zero. Both in autumn and winter the aurora borealis is very active. At the end of March, sunrise and sunset meet and on May seventeenth the arctic day begins. The sun remains continuously in the sky and nature awakens rapidly. Already at the beginning of June the grass comes up. However, even in summer the temperature never rises above fifteen degrees. The inhabitants of Novaya Zemlya are Samoyeds or Samya, cousins of the Eskimos of Greenland, Siberia, and North America. They were settled on the island by the Russian Imperial Government in 1848. Previously the island had been quite empty. The Skete of Saint Nicholas was a missionary venture. It disappeared during the Revolution. Khrushchev used Novaya Zemlya as the testing ground for the most destructive hydrogen bombs and was appalled by the results. Compared with Novaya Zemlya, the neighboring Petchenga seems almost semitropical.

While the Skete of Saint Nicholas was a recent foundation, Petchenga Monastery was not. It was founded in 1533 by Saint Trifon, who evangelized the Laplanders. In 1590, on Christmas Day, Swedish pirates attacked the monastery, killed all the monks, looted the church and burned all the buildings. The surviving monks, those who were absent from the monastery during the massacre, moved to Kola in the eastern part of Russian Lapland and founded a new monastery there. Only in 1886 was Petchenga Monastery restored and it developed very rapidly. At the beginning of the present century there were about fifty professed monks and one hundred and fifty novices, postulants and oblates. In 1920 the Soviet Government surrendered to Finland the small district in which Petchenga Monastery was situated. In this way Petchenga escaped the fate of other Russian monasteries: suppression by the Soviet Government. Just before the Second World War there were still twenty monks in the monastery, all of them from Russia's Far North. During the last war the monks were evacuated to Konevitsa where I found the few survivors.

The Far North always reminds me of that joyous and yet slightly sad state of mind described as *radosto-pechalie*; for want of better words, 'joyfully sad.' All the beauty of those endless forests and numberless lakes, still and deep, I appreciated in Konevitsa. The Far North, more than any other place on earth, gives one the impression of the nearness of the invisible city of God.

Father John was, like a true son of the Far North, *radosto-pechalie*, joyous, calm, contemplative. He was not a great talker, immersed as he was in contemplation and prayer.

Once, I asked him: "Father, tell me, is it true that in order to be saved, to live in God, we must live away from crowds, as you do here in the North?"

He answered: "I believe it is true, man of God. It is very difficult to lead a holy life in the world. There is so much activity and so much vanity. When the devil wants to detach someone from the one thing necessary, he occupies him with a lot of work which does not leave him a free moment for meditation or for deepening his interior life. As a result, the prayer of one who lives in the world is full of distractions, dry and tedious. He may even give up prayer altogether. Such a man is 'drowned' in the world. Of course, men can be saved in the world but it is so much more difficult. The early monks went to the desert in order to be alone with God. It is very difficult indeed to serve God and the world at the same time but such is unavoidable when one lives in the world."

I asked if the Prayer of Jesus could assist such a one.

Father replied that it could but in order to practice the Prayer seriously one really needs solitude, silence and concentration. These are hardly attainable in the world with its vanities, noises and passions which blind men and push them into sins and crimes. Blessed is the man whom the Lord calls to live and to pray to him in these northern forests. When the Kingdom of God comes, all 'practical' activities will disappear. The only occupation of the blessed will be unceasing praise of the glory of God, like unto that of the angels and saints even now before the throne of God in heaven.

I told Father John how I lived for a while in the province of Nizhny-Novgorod where Lake Svetly Yar is situated with which the legend of the City of Kitiesh is associated. People are strongly aware of an invisible presence at Lake Svetly Yar. Now I felt this even more strongly at Konevitsa. I asked Father if people did not feel this even more in Petchenga or in Novaya Zemlya.

"The invisible world, Sergei Nikolaevitch," he answered, "surrounds us everywhere but it is easier to sense its presence when we are in solitude than among crowds."

I remembered and spoke to Father about one night many years before when I was traveling in the Far North. The absolute stillness of that night with its myriad of brilliant stars overawed me. And then the incredibly beautiful aurora borealis began to display its arches and curtains of all colors, hovering over and illuminating the pure white snow. It was like entering into the invisible world of eternity where there is neither time nor space.

Father John's face was serious. "And did you feel a special joy, surpassing all understanding?" he asked.

"Yes, I believe I did."

"Well, then, blessed are you, my dear friend. You are on the right path. You may suffer, you may hesitate but you will move in the right direction. True wisdom is very simple. Always keep your peace of mind. You can do that only by accepting everything God sends you and not wishing for anything else. Father Theophan of the Pskovo-Petchersky Monastery told me this: 'If we meditate seriously on our life, we readily see how the hand of God has led us through even the most difficult circumstances.' It is only an experience such as this that makes our faith solid as a rock. The speculations of the rationalists and the wise ones of this world lead us nowhere and may very well destroy our faith."

As the time for my departure was drawing near, I asked Father John for a word of life. "Father," I said, "I shall soon be leaving the Northland, the gateway to the invisible city of God. What instruction would you offer me?"

Father said very simply: "The invisible city, as you yourself declared, speaking of Kitiesh, is our heart. We must retire there for prayer and meditation. At first we can manage to do this only from time to time but with practice we will be able to abide there continually."

This seemed impossible to me, so I objected. "But, to do that, one must retire to a remote monastery or skete. How could one do such a thing in the world?"

"One can," replied the holy monk. "Father John of Kronstadt, a saintly priest and preacher, my fellow countryman from the province of Arkhangelsk, lived a most strenuous active life and yet he was a great man of prayer and contemplation. It is difficult but not impossible. As you practice the Prayer of Jesus, say it slowly and patiently. Do not hurry, as many do, for that comes to nothing. Time itself will bring results: peace of mind and detachment. You will find then that you have indeed mastered yourself.

"And there is something else that it is important to observe: avoid noise and publicity. Do your work in such a way that your left hand does not know what your right hand is doing. Do not run after people. You will not find either security or justice in them but only in

God. To enter the invisible city, you must be pure of heart as it is justly said of those who wish to enter Kitiesh. For such purity of heart all of us must strive, Sergei Nikolaevitch. May God lead us both in his way. Amen."

CHAPTER 15

Father Luke

ather Luke, guestmaster of New Valamo, was not only very friendly but also deeply spiritual. He had been guestmaster for many years while the community was still in Valaam. He well knew how to deal with people and what to say. I spoke with him chiefly about the monastic tradition of Valaam. One day, I asked him what the celebrated hegumen of Valaam, Staretz Nazary, used to teach about prayer. In response he gave me a little book to read. I read:

> When you are standing in the church and you cannot hear well what is sung or read then say devoutly the Prayer of Jesus. Try your best to implant this Prayer firmly in your soul and heart. Say the Prayer in your mind. Do not allow it to leave your lips. Unite it with your breathing. Bring yourself to heartfelt sorrow and, if you are able, to tears. Do this always. Keep silence and restrain your mind from distractions and artful and cunning thoughts. Persevere always in this way with humility and penance, waiting till Divine Grace overshadows and illumines you.
>
> When you leave the church to go to your cell continue to say the Prayer of Jesus. And in your cell go on with the Jesus Prayer, using your prayer cord. Any old man, any sick person can do that. Remain in prayer and in silence in your cell.

When some particular manual labor is not prescribed, read or undertake some handicraft. When you leave your cell, do not engage in vain talk with the people you meet on your way. If you are able, eat only once a day. When you are serving table in the refectory, always let your face and eyes witness to a heart that is joyful. When you are not serving, take one of the lower seats, if possible even the last.

When I finished the book, I returned it to Father Luke and we discussed the matter. "In this little book everything is so simple, Father Luke."

"If you live simply you will live to be a hundred," Father Luke answered. He went on to say that in the world everything is complicated and confused but for the monk everything is simple. Anyone who practices the Prayer of Jesus must live simply because only a simple life enables one to avoid sin. Staretz Nazary taught that we must always watch over ourselves because passion always begins with something small, hardly observable, but then grows and multiplies exceedingly. We must especially watch over our belly because tasty and pleasant food, washed down with strong drink, leads us straight to gluttony, sensual living and drunkenness which in turn excite our sexuality. This is most contrary to the commitment of the monk and dangerous also for secular clergy and laity alike because it can only lead to vice and ill health.

I told Father Luke of an Anglican clergyman who died at the age of one hundred and four and celebrated in church on the very day of his death. When people asked him to what he attributed his longevity, he used to remain silent, but finally he said:

I believe when we are young we may eat as much as we can. Later we should be satisfied with what is given to us but after seventy we must eat little and less and less every year.

Father Luke replied: "This is wise, my friend. Bishop Isidore, Metropolitan of Novgorod, St. Petersburg and Finland, who died in office at the age of ninety-three, always gave this answer to those who were astonished at his age and abilities:

> The secret of this health, my dear fathers and brothers, is simple. I was never over worried about anything. We are pilgrims who have no abiding city but look for the world to come. We must not be attached, therefore, to anything earthly and transitory. Saint John Damascene writes in the same vein in his Office of the Dead. What worldly pleasure is free from sorrow? What glory on this earth remains unchanged? Everything is a passing shadow, a dream and an illusion. In a single moment death destroys all that.

"Father Nazary was right in saying that no one who intends to lead an ascetic life can avoid sorrows and troubles. Because people naturally do not want to face unchallengeable truth, they prefer to harbor the illusion that there will be no retribution for their passions and vices. They hate those whose lives condemn them. This happens even in monasteries. A monk hardly begins to lead a truly ascetic life before the devil begins to make trouble for him. Sometimes it comes from his superiors, sometimes from those who are living indifferent lives. They will start to speak of him with irony: 'Look what a holy man has appeared! A hypocrite! A fool!' When this happens he must remain silent, be humble and keep the Prayer of Jesus on his lips and in his heart. He must not become discouraged, remembering the multitude of his sins, and he must receive with gratitude the humiliations that heal his weaknesses."

As Father shared all this, I could not help but think and even say, "But this is hard, Father Luke."

"Who says that it is easy? With us in Valaam, those who practiced the Prayer of Jesus were advised to go to their spiritual father for daily confession of thoughts. Father Nazary said this:

After the evening meal go to your spiritual father, bow before him, kneel and open to him the state of your soul during the day just ended, describing all you did in deed and in word, how you thought ill of people, how you were given to vanity and pride, how you offended your brothers or were offended by them and condemned them. Try to watch over your most insignificant thoughts which disturb the purity and peace of your soul. If you cannot remember everything, note things down on paper. After confession and receiving absolution, which comes as it were from God himself, kiss the cross and the icon and prostrate yourself before the staretz and then return to your cell. Continue to recite in your mind, while walking, the Prayer of Jesus and diligently avoid all meetings and conversations in order not to be scandalized or to scandalize others. When you reach your cell, make your thanksgiving, read for a time and then stand up for the night vigil."

I remarked that it seemed to me that such a life is possible only in monasteries where there is a staretz but not in the world.

Father agreed that in the world one must have another rule. Yet with a daily confession of thoughts everything goes on much quicker. We must make progress not only in prayer but also in keeping guard over our thoughts.

Father Luke then told me that Father Nazary gave the following advice for when one prayed alone:

First of all, lift up your mind and your heart to God and realize to whom you pray. Watch that your thoughts do not wander here and there. Lay aside your preoccupations with worldly things.

After that, in deep silence and serenity of heart, stand before the icon, incline your head, cross your hands on your breast, place your feet close together and close your eyes. Pray mentally, let the tears flow, give vent to sighs, reproach yourself. Repent, ask God to forgive all your sins, weep.

Observe what psalms influence you most, bring you to deep sorrow, arouse your feelings, calling forth tears. Use those psalms often. Nevertheless, do not become anxious. It is not important to read or to sing everything prescribed; what is important is to read or sing with feeling, tenderness and sorrow of heart.

If obedience and duty call you away, go in peace. Do not feel guilty about reducing your private prayer. In old age and in sickness, pray as you can, sitting or lying down, and reproach yourself: Well, I am old now and ill. I am not able to pray as I ought and to thank God for his great mercies to me, unworthy and sick.

I had heard that Staretz Agapy, who was a teacher of prayer, had also been there, and inquired about him.

"Yes, he lived in Valaam and taught many monks, just as Father Nazary did." And then Father Luke went on to speak at length of Father Agapy's teaching. Perhaps with even greater insistence, Father Agapy used to say that prayer at first is difficult. Only by forming ourselves through practice can we hope to acquire it. But if we have a firm resolution to become men of prayer, its practice becomes easier and easier. Finally, we become even irresistibly attracted to it. In vocal prayer we must pronounce all the words slowly, meditatively, concentrating our attention on the thoughts expressed in the words of the prayer. When our mind is distracted by alien thoughts we must return, without annoyance or depression, to the words of our prayer.

"Wholeness of mind comes slowly, not when we want it but when we become humble and when God gives it to us. We attain to undistracted prayer neither by time nor by the number of prayers we say, as some people believe, but by a humble heart, by continuous effort to pray well and by grace. Attentive vocal prayer, of itself, passes on to mental prayer.

"Prayer is called 'mental' when we approach God with only the mind or when we contemplate God. But when we pray mentally we must keep our attention in the heart; that is, we must pray with feeling. In due course the Lord will grant us, for our humility and labor, a wholeness and concentration in prayer. When our attention to the Lord becomes continuous, it is called 'attention by grace' because our own attention is always supported by God's grace.

"With the help of an experienced staretz, our mental prayer will gradually transform itself into the interior Prayer of the Heart. The Prayer of the Heart is that prayer in which we feel in our heart that we are with God and our heart is fired with love for him. He who wants to practice prayer rightly must, according to the Gospel, deny his own will and human reasoning and take up the cross: endure patiently all the hardships, spiritual and bodily, that are a necessary part of the ascetic life."

"What is the place of heart, Father Luke? How does one bring about a union between mind and heart?" I asked.

Father patiently answered my questions, explaining that when an ascetic gives himself up entirely to Divine Providence and humbles himself and is ready to endure the work of prayer, the Lord God, in due course, brings to an end the man's efforts and stabilizes his mind and heart with the abiding memory of God in his heart. When such a state of mind becomes perpetual and as it were natural, this is the union of mind and heart. This is truly unceasing prayer without words or images. In this state the mind does not want to wander about and if by business or much talking it is precluded from dwelling in the heart, it is irresistibly drawn to return to itself and to continue building the interior cell. In such a state everything in us passes on from the head to the heart, from discursive reason to intention; all leads to spiritual enlightenment. Then an incomprehensible spiritual light illumines the ascetic and bathes him inwardly in light. Everything that he thinks and does, he does now with entire consciousness and attention. It is a transfiguration. The pray-er then sees from whence come his thoughts, intentions, and desires. He is able then to force his reason, heart and will to obey Christ and to fulfill the will of God and to carry out the command of the Fathers. If he transgresses, he at once redeems his fault with true penance and humbly prostrates himself before God who has pity and continues to supply the ascetic with his grace. All this can be understood only by personal experience. Contemplation comes when a heart is altogether purified. The ascetic then realizes his utter insignificance before God and continually sees his own sinfulness. These sentiments of poverty and unceasing penance are accompanied by a constant expectation of death, judgment and the eternal sentence. The ascetic meditates on the life of Christ, his Passion and his teaching as they are described in the Holy Scriptures and explained by the Fathers. Finally, he contemplates the divine attributes: omniscience, omnipotence, wisdom, goodness, love of men and women, justice and long-suffering. Father Agapy corresponded with Bishop Theophan the Recluse and asked his advice. The bishop believed that the most important thing is to live in the Presence of God, remembering him always. The Prayer of the Heart is therefore a prayer of humble sentiments or penance with the continual remembrance of the all-present God who sees everything. This produces in us fear and piety. All the rest, such as the inclination of the head, sitting on a low chair, breathing, et cetera, are nothing more than methods which add nothing essential. We may say prayers while we are walking or sitting but in the cell it is better to pray with metanias or deep bows.

"There is a 'prayer without words.' This means we remain continually in prayerful sentiments toward God without pronouncing words with our lips or in our mind and, of course, without any images. According to Bishop Theophan, this is the supreme degree of prayer. Only such a prayer can be unceasing.

"This is the teaching of our men of prayer. If you want to learn more," Father Luke added, "our Staretz, Father Michael, might tell you. He has been a hermit and recluse and obtained the rare gift of tears of grace."

I met Father Luke once more, in 1960, in Pskovo-Petchersky Monastery, when I visited the Soviet Union. He then lived with Father Michael in a separate house with a chapel, the one in which I visited Father Pimen in 1926. The house is surrounded by a garden. Father Luke met me at the entrance. He was now bent with years but as friendly as before and very evidently filled with the Holy Spirit. His words were crisp: "Well, we meet again, my dear friend. You still search for spiritual wisdom? Search and you will find it. Did you visit Mount Athos? Did you see Father Ilian? A long time ago, he visited us in Valaam. I heard that he is a true staretz now. Did you come to see Father Michael? Come along."

After my conversation with Father Michael, I said but a few words to Father Luke. I was in a hurry to return to Leningrad. Father Luke died some years later, at the age of ninety-three. Bishops, crowds of clergy and a multitude of lay folk from Moscow, Leningrad and even farther away came to his burial. This ended the witness of the last of the surviving Valaam startzy who came with Father Michael to Pskovo-Petchersky Monastery from Finland in 1957.

CHAPTER 16

Father John of Petchenga

In the course of my visit to New Valamo I had several long talks with Father John. He was at that time confessor of the community. He had been hegumen of Petchenga. In particular I remember one afternoon, still and sunny. One sensed already the approach of the long northern winter although it was only the second half of August. The air was clear and pure, free of all pollution. The shadows were sharp and the water in the lake pale blue. White cloudlets chased each other across a pale blue sky. The wonderful silence of the North reigned around us. This was truly a spot for prayer and meditation, far away from the crowds, noise, and dirt of the cities.

I greeted the hegumen and received his blessing. "It is very fine here, Father John. It is so quiet and so remote."

"This is nothing compared to Petchenga," answered the monk.

Petchenga is truly remote. In winter it is totally isolated. There is nothing but the snow-covered tundra and the distant roar of the ocean in the background. It is the case even now. But what it was like in the sixteenth century when Saint Trifon, the Apostle of the Lapps, first arrived there and founded the monastery, is beyond description. In those days Petchenga was remote indeed. Saint Seraphim of Sarov used to say, "Solitude, prayer, charity and abstinence are the four wheels of the chariot that carries the spirit to heaven." In Petchenga one has every opportunity to practice these four virtues. Solitude is indeed present; there are no human habitations for miles. Solitude with its silence promotes true prayer, undistracted, attentive, sober. There is every opportunity to practice charity for the Lapps come from time to time to the monastery either to pray or to ask for something. Finally, in the rude conditions of the tundra with its cold and darkness and its infertility one may practice abstinence to one's heart's content.

I told the hegumen how I once lived for a time in the Russian North. I loved it: the great silence, especially at night, the wonderful aurora borealis, the starry skies, the virgin snow and the great dark forest. But the tundra I always found depressing and Father John agreed. In the Far North only really good monks can survive, those with true prayer of the heart. In the milder climates, there are many pleasing distractions: the change of seasons, the flowers, singing birds, wild beasts. But not so in the Far North: there is the monotonous, nine-month-long winter with a night that lasts three months and then a short and rather hot summer when the tundra turns into an immense marshy land with clouds of mosquitoes that torment men and animals without respite. Only perfectly balanced men with true peace of mind who are able to pray and meditate continuously can survive. They are helped by the fact that there is manual work and plenty of it: orchards, fishing, the herds of reindeer, and so on.

I had recently met a scientist who spent several years in Antarctica, where the climatic conditions are worse than in Petchenga or even in Novaya Zemlya, the skete beyond the Arctic Circle. He was working with a scientific expedition. They lived in houses under the snow. Although rude and simple, these houses were quite comfortable and well heated. They allowed the men to persevere in their scientific observations and experiments. I asked him whether he liked Antarctica and whether he would like to return. To my astonishment he said that he liked it greatly and would not mind returning to it. The great attraction of Antarctica, this scientist said, lay in its incomparable silence and solitude. The air is pure and invigorating. There is no smoke from factory chimneys, no exhaust fumes from cars, no noise. During the day the blinding white of the snow and the blue sky and at night the starry sky and the display of the wonderful aurora australis. And there is also life, especially along the coast: crowds of penguins, all kinds of birds, whales and other sea creatures. In Antarctica one naturally tends to live in astonishment before the grandeur of the cosmos and to meditate on the indescribable power and wisdom of God. I asked this scientist whether the monastic life would be possible in Antarctica. "Why not?" he answered. "If scientists can live there, monks can live there too, and more easily because they are more accustomed to live an interior life. Of course, they must have some occupation; they could conduct scientific observations and experiments."

When I stayed two years ago in Boquen Abbey in Brittany, its founder, my old friend Abbot Alexis Presse, told me about the celebrated French scientist and Nobel prizewinner, Alexis Carrel. At the end of his life, Carrel returned to the Christian faith after years in the religious wilderness. This scientist had dreamed of the foundation of a religious community that would support itself not by agriculture or industry but by scientific research. I asked the hegumen if he thought such a thing might be possible. "Why not? Every work done for God or one's neighbor is good. Scientific research is good, if pursued with humility."

I went on to ask Father John why Russian monks always moved toward the North. It was his conviction that they started to move from the Kiev area to the North after the Mongol invasion had devastated the country there and everyone felt insecure. Religious life, if properly lived, demands solitude, peace and silence. What peace could there be if raiders could be expected to arrive at any moment to kill and loot? But the Mongols could not penetrate the great northern forests. There was nothing to loot there. In the North there was security. So the monks moved to the North, always farther and farther, till at length they crossed the Arctic Circle. Of course, perfect security is not of this world. Even Petchenga was looted from time to time by Scandinavian pirates and Lapp marauders. The same happened to Valaam, but Solovky was so remote and so inaccessible that it remained intact until the Bolshevik Revolution when it was turned into a prison.

I wondered if now, when the world is so quickly filling up with people and solitude is harder and harder to find, the same trend might not begin again. Father thought it quite possible. "Those who really love solitude can find it at its best in the polar regions, remote, harsh, and barely accessible. But even there one must live quietly; otherwise the curious will come. They started to flock even to Petchenga in the last years before the Second World War. Still, we must always remember that the most important solitude is inner solitude."

"What is inner solitude?" I asked. And Father John replied most beautifully. "Inner solitude is God and the soul, nothing more." He continued by asking what benefit is it for us to dwell in external solitude if we have our minds continually occupied with worldly thoughts and passions? Distractions and vain, wandering thoughts come because in our innermost selves we do not believe in the presence of God everywhere. He whose thoughts wander about even in church can hardly be called a devout Christian. All our troubles come about because of the absence within us of the fear of God. The Far North is a good teacher of the fear of God. In those endless snow-covered plains, where there is no town or village, we are confronted with eternal and unchangeable facts. The night sky, clear and dark, is lit up with myriads of stars and the mysterious aurora borealis.

Father asked me if I had seen this magnificent phenomenon. Yes I had, many times, I said, and that it was an awe inspiring spectacle with many colored arches, curtains, and cascades, all silent and beautiful. In the face of such splendor one feels so small, puny, utterly insignificant.

"There, my dear Sergei Nikolaevitch, is the beginning of the fear of God, this sentiment or sensation of the utter nothingness of oneself and of the incomprehensible power and glory of God." Father went on to point out that in the towns we hardly see nature. We are surrounded on all sides with the wonders of our own technological creations. But how insignificant they are seen to be when compared with the abysses of God's creation! Living among the things we have made makes us proud and arrogant. We begin to believe we are the master of the universe, a genius, leading brute and unthinking nature to perfection. This is a dangerous illusion, similar to that of Satan. We want to be God but we are not. We are merely very insignificant creatures lost in the enormous spaces of the cosmos. Father said he often meditated on this when he was in Petchenga.

"It would be fine to found a monastery in the Far North, Father, like your Petchenga or the Skete of Novaya Zemlya," I mused. "Yes," he agreed, "it would be but for the time being it is hardly possible." He went on to explain that they could not found a monastery in Finnish Lapland because they were so few and old. Since the Soviet troops occupied Petchenga, the little community has been in exile. Some were in New Konevitsa and some were at New Valamo. New Konevitsa had so few monks that it was on the point of disappearing. Father expected the surviving monks would join the little group at New Valamo. And then the end of New Valamo itself would be near. It seemed to be but a question of time. The Orthodox Church of Finland has hardly more than seventy thousand members and it is unable to maintain three monasteries. Moreover, the spirit of its clergy is far from favoring the monastic. No monastery could be founded in the Soviet North, which stretches from Finland to Alaska.

"Perhaps one could be founded in Alaska or Canada," I conjectured. Father doubted this. There were nearly five million Orthodox in North America of many ethnic origins, with the Greeks forming the largest group. But the monastic spirit was absent. The Greeks have been unable to found a single monastery of their own. The Russians of the Metropolia have Saint Tikhon's Monastery in Pennsylvania but it is not a flourishing community. The Russian traditionalists have a good monastery in Jordanville, New York, but it is very active, not contemplative, and in the Far North only the latter would do. The flourishing skete that exists in Boston today was not yet in existence. Still, Father hoped it might happen one day. A movement is on foot to canonize the Valaam Staretz Herman who died in 1837 in Alaska. The Alaskan mission was founded by the Valaam community at the end of the eighteenth century.

I then asked, "Could hermits exist in the Far North, Father?"

"I doubt it very much," he replied. "Life in those frozen tundras is very harsh indeed. The cold is intense and it lasts many months. Houses must be well heated in order simply to survive and food must be plentiful and nourishing. And then there is the great northern loneliness. It might well bring on deep melancholy. Father Jonah told me that. He had come from Valaam where there was a large community, a beautiful view, a great lake, fine forests with a lot of animals. In Petchenga he found the endless tundra and the long nights monotonous and depressing."

Father John went on: "It is hard to live in a small community cheek by jowl. It is perhaps harder than to live alone. Only monks with a deep and settled interior life should go to the Far North, those for whom only God matters. For them the Far North is a true paradise. One rapidly acquires the fear of God, a sense of awe and adoration while contemplating a starry sky, the aurora borealis or the frightful storms in the glacial ocean. And the fear of God is the beginning of all wisdom. Naturally it is easier to acquire continuous prayer of the heart in the Far North. There are no distractions. Attention is easily concentrated. One really needs to experience all this for oneself."

Father went on, speaking softly and slowly: "God is within us. In the world, because our attention is continually distracted, it takes a long time to find him. In the Far North it is easy. Indeed the Far North is the same desert as that of the Egyptian hermits, except it is covered with snow. In the Far North continuous prayer is very restful because it saves us from daydreaming, something very common when life is monotonous. Daydreaming usually leads to illusions which are very dangerous in the loneliness of the Far North.

"Remember," Father said, "no one can approach God before he leaves the 'world.' The 'world,' according to the Fathers, is the totality of passions. When they live within us we are still in the world. To purify ourselves from these passions, we must enter into our inner chamber and throw them out by prayer and ascetic living. Those who think they can master their passions and the sins born of them without continuous prayer and hard living delude themselves. We can save ourselves anywhere in any situation, provided we pray continually and live soberly. If we do this we can master the very devils, as Christ himself told the Apostles. The Far North merely offers a better situation in which to practice continuous prayer of the heart and abstemious living."

The bell in the tower started to ring. "It is time to go to church for vespers," Father John said as he stood up. We went to the church.

I had another discussion with Father John on the monastic life in the Far North. It took place in the morning, after Liturgy out by the lake. I told Father of the great Volga forests, of the skete on Kerzhenetz, of Staretz Zosima Verkhovsky, elements of whose life were used by Dostoevsky in his *Brothers Karamazov* to depict Staretz Zosima.

"Many people," Father John said wisely, "have romantic ideas about monastic life and the Far North. That is not good. When they meet the hard realities of life, they become despondent and unhappy. In life we must never set our hearts on any kind of blessedness. That awaits us in the world to come. We must, on the contrary, look on our life as the way of the cross, as a merited penance for our sins. The Fathers say: 'Pray well and expect the worst.' It is obvious the more progress we make in prayer and ascetic living the more excited the devil becomes and he then plays all kinds of tricks on us."

I asked a final question: "How can we find our way in life, Father?"

"The very circumstances of our life show us the way; also the advice of God-fearing people and the intimations of our religious superiors. We must never follow our own inclinations and choose the things that appear to us best and most desirable. It is here that danger lies in wait for us. If you would go to the Far North to satisfy your fancy, then do not go; but if you are sent, then, indeed, do go. I was sent to Petchenga. It was my duty to go."

It is these very simple and humble words that have remained with me as the fruit of my encounter with Father John of Petchenga.

One day in the month of August I was again sitting in the garden of New Valamo Monastery with Father John. Even with the sun and a certain heat, we could already feel the approach of winter. The air was quite clear, even in the shade, and the calm morning was all golden.

"Tell me, Father John, are variations allowed in the Jesus Prayer, or not?" I asked.

"They exist. Indeed, the demon tempts you everywhere. We say that there is one demon attached to every layman, two to a monk and three to the one who practices the Jesus Prayer. Have you read the *Anthology on the Jesus Prayer* and *The Conversations about the Jesus Prayer*, published by our late Abbot Chariton?"

"Yes, I have read them."

"He speaks about this subject. His main point is that the one who practices the Jesus Prayer must be a humble person. Some people think too highly of themselves. Why do we recite the Jesus Prayer? That we may continuously remember the Lord and by repentance gain serenity of soul, inner silence, love of Truth and of our neighbor. Then we live in God, who is love. There are some people, however, who consider the Jesus Prayer a sort of magic operation that can provide them with wonderful things, for example, the ability to read the thoughts of others, the prediction of events, the gift of healing, and so on. Such an approach must be condemned. Those who think this way easily become the victims of demons who give them a certain occult power in order to destroy them for ever.

"I was the Abbot of Petchenga. It is very far from here, on the shores of the Arctic Ocean. During summer the sun does not set for three months but in winter the night also lasts three months. The

111

solitude is almost absolute and the tempestuous ocean and the tundra all around are empty and sad. In such conditions, some monks become manic and start to hear voices and to have visions. One monk started to hear, in his cell, the voices of would-be angels who suggested to him that he had become a saint and that he could, like our Lord, walk on the sea. Convinced by these voices, our illuminated monk decided to prove to himself their truth and he tried to walk on thin ice, like an angel with no weight. He was saved but he died shortly afterwards from the consequences of his immersion in ice-cold water. This is an extreme case but the demons tempt wiser men differently. By praying a lot and by observing within themselves a certain spiritual progress, certain people come gradually and imperceptibly to believe that they are very good and they start to despise others as carnal and unworthy of their profession. Finally, they arrive at the opinion that they are the very elect of God with a mission to correct and teach others. Such people criticize everyone, are easily irritable when blamed by others and they are always worried. It is true that the Apostle Paul said that whoever invokes the Lord Jesus Christ for his salvation and confesses that he is the Son of God will be saved but the Lord himself also explained: 'Not every one who says, "Lord, Lord," shall enter into the Kingdom of heaven but he that does the will of my Father who is in heaven.' These people invoke the Lord but their heart is far from him. We must therefore add to the Prayer the practice of virtues because faith without works is dead. It is by works that faith comes to perfection."

"How can we recognize, Father, the one to whom we can turn to receive advice?"

"Search for a serene staretz, good and humble, who lives with inner silence and who has a conscience without reproach; that is one who judges no one and scandalizes no one. Always avoid those who criticize everybody, those who are always unhappy and especially those who are avaricious. We must flee from these people otherwise we ourselves will become corrupted if we stay with them. Remember also that it is good to live with a staretz for a certain time to learn the Prayer and watchfulness of the heart but when you have learnt all this, to what ends can a staretz serve you? We must not always live like a little child. With age we must answer personally for our sins and our foolishness. When the time comes you yourself may become a staretz."

"How is that?"

"It is very simple. The staretz or elder is a man rich in spiritual experiences, wisdom coming from God and of a great love for humankind. Several simple monks became great startzy, such as Staretz Zosima Verkhovsky, of whom Dostoevsky wrote a portrait in his Staretz Zosima of *The Brothers Karamazov*; Staretz Vasilisk of Turinsk; Father John of Moldavia and the Elder Melchizedek, the hermit of the Roslavi Forest, who died at the age of one hundred and twenty-five. Daniel of Atchinsk, a great Siberian staretz, and Kosmas of Birsk were simple laymen. In spite of this they were visited not only by other laymen and by secular priests but also by monks, by bishops of great wisdom and even by other startzy. And what a great staretz the anonymous peasant was who wrote *The Way of a Pilgrim*. We have found in the correspondence of Father Ambrose of Optino that he was a peasant from Orel.

"As the manuscript of *The Way* was discovered at the Monastery of Saint Panteleimon on Mount Athos, it is possible that the original of the manuscript may be found there. Perhaps this Pilgrim on his way back from the Holy Land to Russia visited Mount Athos as many pilgrims did. He may have told his story to the Confessor of the Monastery, the great Hieroschimonk Jerome Solomentsev. Father Jerome may have ordered another monk to write *The Way*. Perhaps the author wrote it himself. Who knows?"

"Is the way of pilgrimage an heroic act, Father John?"

"Undoubtedly. Only the Fool for Jesus Christ is above it. But the practice of being a Fool for Jesus Christ is not permitted unless with the blessing of a great staretz. It is only with great effort that we can support the practice of the ordinary virtues and so how could we dare to practice foolishness for the sake of Jesus Christ? They tell the following story of Staretz Leonid of Optino. A monk wanted to wear chains. Father Leonid disapproved of this custom. He told the monk that salvation did not depend on wearing chains. The staretz answered him: 'Why wear chains? Monastic life is itself a heavy enough chain to carry if it is lived correctly.' However, the monk persisted. Finally, the staretz decided to silence him. He called the monastery's smith and told him: 'When a certain brother comes to ask you to make chains for him, tell him: "What do you want chains for?" And then strike him hard in the face.' After a short time the staretz said to the monk: 'All right, go to the smith and ask him to make the chains for you.' The monk ran happily to the smith and said to him: 'The staretz has given permission for chains to be made for me.' The smith, very busy at the time, said: 'What do you want chains for?' and struck him hard in the face. The angry monk struck the smith in his turn and both came to the staretz. Acquitting the smith, the staretz said to the monk: 'How can you dare to wear chains when you are unable to endure a mere slap in the face? You must not try to jump over your own head.'"

"Father Michael told me: 'Sow, my friend, the good word everywhere, on the roads, on the stones, in the wilderness. Maybe something will grow and bear fruit a hundredfold.' What do you think of this, Father John?"

"Well, if Father Michael told you that, you must obey him. Sow the good word and you will be that Pilgrim, a stranger everywhere. It is, my friend, a heavy burden."

"Will I be able to carry it, Father?"

"With faith, you can, because the Apostle Paul has said: 'I can do all things through Christ who strengthens me.' Attach yourself to the Jesus Prayer, it will help you."

CHAPTER 17

Father Nektari

I met Father Nektari in Uusi Valamo, Finland, in the summer of 1954. I was walking on the shore of the lake near the monastery and meditating over the letters of the celebrated Staretz Ambrose of Optino. The day was warm and sunny. The slight southern wind was pleasant. Little white clouds occasionally crossed the sky. All around the deep silence of the Great North reigned. The fresh green grass of the meadows was embroidered with many flowers. The lake reflected the blue sky and the green forest on the coast.

"God bless you, man of God," a friendly monk with a grey beard and blue eyes greeted me. "I hear you go for talks to Father Michael, our recluse. That is good. He is a saintly man. They are rare nowadays. He suffered a lot in the past for his resistance to various modernist tendencies but this is now over. We should really return to Russia, where monks are badly needed. Father Michael thinks so. We are only refugees here. It is time to find eternal rest in the mother country."

"But, Father, there is the atheist government."

"And what of that? Many foes invaded Russia or ruled over it throughout history and oppressed the Church. The Mongols were our overlords for over two hundred years and were very cruel but they didn't touch the Church. The Poles, the Swedes, the French and the Germans penetrated Russia deeply and often behaved worse than the Mongols but they all left. Our own people were often worse than the foreigners in their relations with the Church. Ivan the Terrible murdered a good many Christians in Novgorod and elsewhere. Some people murdered by him were canonized, for example Saint Philip, Metropolitan of Moscow, and Saint Cornelius, Abbot of Pskovo-Petchersky Monastery. Peter the Great oppressed the Church, abolished the Patriarchate of Moscow and replaced it by a synod obedient to him. The oppression became worse under the Empress Anne, while Catherine II secularized the Church's properties and closed down many monasteries. The Communists of course oppress the Church more than anybody else and made millions of martyrs but, on the other hand, they are declared atheists while many former oppressors posed as Orthodox and even as fervently Orthodox."

"I have read about all that, Father Nektari."

"That is good," the monk answered. "We must try to attain peace of soul and to practice the Jesus Prayer, as Father Michael does and then everything will come right by itself. Here we are merely refugees from the old Valaam. There was piety and holy living under the late Emperor. Then Finland became independent and the Bolsheviks became masters of Russia.

"We were separated from the Russian God-fearing masses. Novices disappeared and the community began to age. Then there was a new war and we were evacuated here. Around us are the Lutherans, and the Orthodox Finns are a small minority. In Russia there is now a spiritual revival but there is a great lack of clergy and even more of monks. Therefore there is a great need of those who can spread our faith."

"But how can you do it, Father? The teaching of religion is forbidden at schools and prevented at home. Printing religious books is hindered. The Church cannot use the modern media, wireless or television. Nothing is allowed except church services."

"That is enough. If someone celebrates church services well and lives in Christ, he attracts people to the Church by his example, by his very life. It is much better than learned dissertations and scholarly discussions."

Once, walking with Father Nektari in the forest, I asked him how we could know the will of God in some business if we have not a staretz or experienced spiritual father to consult.

"You ask a difficult question, Sergei Nikolaevitch. The ancient Fathers advised us in such cases to pray three times to the Lord that he would reveal his will to us. We should make such prayers for three days and take the first suggestion appearing in our heart as a Divine answer and, accepting this with firm faith, act accordingly. The Fathers called this the answer of the heart. If, before asking Divine guidance in prayer, we decide to act according to our reason, we might commit grievous mistakes. It is better to say such prayers once daily for three days but in case of extreme need we can say them one after another, thrice. The Fathers also said that if a suggestion appears transparently good but our soul is troubled, we should not accept such a suggestion but only that which comes silently and with joy in God. We must also know that suggestions, promising us pleasant things, we accept joyfully, while those offering hardships and sorrows are rejected by us as exceeding our strength or inconvenient to us. Life in Christ is very simple and open to everybody. We must live as the Gospel teaches and as our duties prescribe. Once you live according to the Gospel, you will find out by experience that there is the evil spirit to tempt us. Duty commands us to do one thing while evil suggestions propose something different. Do your duty and don't discuss the evil suggestions because they will offer you many arguments why you shouldn't do your duty and even show you your disobedience as a heroic deed. And when you surrender yourself to evil suggestions and perform the forbidden deed, the wily devil in order to destroy you will immerse you in despair."

"And the evil one, is he crafty, Father?"

"Once you live according to Christ you will find this out quickly. The evil spirits watch us all the time and we must struggle with them. Those who have submitted to evil are not attacked by devils. Why should the devils attack them when they are already in their power? Old criminals are hardly ever tormented by conscience. They have lost it."

In 1957 Father Nektari returned to Russia with Father Michael and his group. He died in Pskovo-Petchersky Monastery.

CHAPTER 18

Father Michael

$\mathbb{F}$ather Michael, the Recluse of Uusi Valamo who died in 1962, was the latest representative of the Valaam mystical tradition. I visited him in 1954 and described my talks with him in various articles and finally in a short book entitled *Father Michael, Recluse of Uusi Valamo*. Father Michael, a native of western Russia, entered Valaam at the beginning of this century. He was for a time attached to Valaam Priory in St. Petersburg. Otherwise he spent all his time in Valaam itself. In the early twenties, when there were divisions in the Valaam community concerning which calendar to observe, the Julian or the Gregorian, he sided with the first group, but the second came into power. Thereupon he retired, first to a skete and then to a hermitage on Smolensky Island.

During the Second World War the Valaam community was transferred to central Finland to Uusi Valamo. Unable to continue his eremitical life in the new surroundings, Father Michael became a recluse. Some years ago Dr. Nicholas Yarushevich, Metropolitan of Krutitsi, the second most important prelate of the Russian Church, visited Valaam. He asked Father Jerome, then abbot of Uusi Valamo, to recommend a monk to him for spiritual guidance, the one whom he considered best. The abbot recommended Father Michael. The Metropolitan spent a long time talking with the recluse. Returning to the abbot, the prelate expressed his wonder and his admiration for the recluse. The Metropolitan asked the abbot to allow people, particularly the clergy, to visit Father Michael for spiritual conversation. Since that time an ever-increasing number of people from all over the world have come to Uusi Valamo to obtain the advice or direction of Father Michael in all kinds of difficulties. This ever-increasing stream of visitors began to tire Father Michael, who was essentially a contemplative. He found himself at eighty years of age in a position not very different from that of the great startzy of Optino. In 1957, when some of the outstanding difficulties which separated the Russian Patriarchate from the Orthodox Church in Finland were overcome, the Metropolitan of Krutitsi once more visited Valamo. He invited Father Michael to come to Russia, where monks like him are badly needed. Father Michael accepted the invitation and on October 15, 1957 he went to Moscow accompanied by seven of his closest friends and disciples, all priest-monks of Uusi Valamo: Father Luke, Father Sergius, Father Gennadius, and four others. The Russian Patriarch gave Father Michael and his disciples the ancient and beautiful Pskovo-Petchersky Monastery near Pskov in western Russia. On the eve of his departure to the Soviet Union Father Michael sent me his last letter of direction. He announced his decision to return to the life of a recluse: "I will give no more direction. The Lord has commanded me to pray fervently for everyone and to lead a hidden life, but not to teach. Like Saint Arsenius the Great, I love everyone and run away from all."

Father Michael belongs to the school of Paissy Velichkovsky. A disciple of the latter, Theodore, lived in Valaam together with Leo Nagolkin, the first great staretz of Optino. They trained Barlaam, later Abbot of Valaam, and Father Euthemius, the confessor of the community. The latter had as his disciples Damaskin, who became abbot of Valaam, and Father Agathangel, who became its confessor. The latter trained Mavriky, another zealot of Valaam, the teacher and spiritual director of Father Michael.

I had altogether five long talks with Father Michael. A peculiarity of Father Michael was that before you could ask him something he already answered you. He knew what you wanted from him. This was, of course, the case with many other startzy. In our first conversation we discussed praying for the dead. Sometime before my meeting with Father Michael I had lost someone dear to me and wanted to ask Father Michael about prayer for the dead. Before I could ask him he took a leaflet from his table and handed it to me. It was entitled *On Commemoration of the Dead*. This leaflet, apparently a sermon he delivered on November 23, 1947, was one of the best vindications of prayer for the dead which I have ever read. The leaflet stressed the need not only for prayer for the dead but also for their commemoration during Liturgy. It states:

> We should continue to truly love our dear dead. When we shall die, they shall remember us at death's hour with the same love with which we commemorate them now. This will help us. While we bid them farewell here with tears and prayers, they will meet us with joy and good tidings. The dead know everything about us and what we do. They see and hear perfectly when we pray for them. Therefore, if you want to help your dead loved one wholeheartedly and do everything commanded by the Holy Church, never allow yourself any doubt about his or her ultimate salvation. Such doubt is a suggestion of the evil spirit. And why? Because if the dead were unworthy of salvation, God would not allow you to pray for them. As St. John Damascene says: "God moves no one to pray for those dead who are unworthy of salvation, neither their parents, nor a wife, nor a husband, nor any relatives or friends." The following prophecy is fulfilled in them: "Miserable are those among the dead for whom none among the living prays."

When I finished reading the paper I looked in wonder at the staretz. His astonishing eyes, bright and clear, looked at me. I realized at once that Father Michael read my thoughts and knew my past.

"Father," I asked him, "what do you think of death?"

"There is no death," he answered, "there is merely a passing from one state to another. To me personally, the life of the other world is much more real than my life here. The more the Christian lives the interior life the more he is detached from this world and imperceptibly he approaches the other world. When the end comes it is easy; the thin veil simply dissolves. Prayers for the dead are needful not only for them but for us as well."

During this first talk we also discussed Divine Providence, the inner life, prayer and repentance. During my second talk with Father Michael on August 12, 1954, I wanted to ask him why a tragedy which I experienced in 1951 had happened. When I came to the staretz, before I could ask him anything, he silently gave me another leaflet to read. When I took it I read: *It Came From Me.*

Happiness and misfortune, rise and fall, health and sickness, glory and dishonor, wealth and poverty, everything comes from me and must be accepted as such. Those who entrust themselves to me and accept all the trials which I send them will not be ashamed on the Day of Judgment. They will realize even here in this world why their life took this course and not another. I send everyone that which is best for him.

During the second talk we discussed many subjects, including miracles, heroic virtues, confession, daily services and mystical states. According to the staretz love is the greatest virtue. "Never judge anyone," he said, "have no foes, revere everyone. In life avoid anything which makes you proud and which disturbs your serenity of mind.

"The best prayer is, as you said yourself, 'Thy will be done.' True repentance covers all sins. Remember always that all troubles in this life are designed to make us more detached in this world. Therefore they lead us to a better life. External piety and devotions, vocal prayers, vigils and fasts are good and needful but only as a frame for an intense inner life of humility, unceasing prayer and trust in God. If the latter are absent, the former are not of much use."

On mystical states Father Michael said that they could be understood only by those who experienced them personally.

"As a blind man," Father Michael said, "cannot picture colors, so an earthly man is unable to picture the wonders perceived in contemplation. These wonders are usually rewards for those who have obtained a spiritual crown. According to Staretz Ambrose of Optino there are five crowns. The most glorious is given for the patient endurance of sorrows. The remaining four are given for virginity, monastic life, spiritual direction of others and sickness borne with resignation. To the five crowns correspond seven heavens. Five of them are reserved for those who follow the Lamb wherever he goes, that is, for the ascetics, mystics and religious, while the other heavens are for the rest. Mind you, all those crowns and heavens signify only various mystical and spiritual states. They are incommunicable. None but those who experienced them personally can understand them."

During our third meeting we discussed the blessed valley of tears, daily celebration of the Liturgy, frequent communion and the Divine will. The staretz fully agreed with Saint Isaac the Syrian that as long as one did not enter into the valley of tears one still served the world, that is, one still led a worldly life and worked for God only outwardly while the inward man remained sterile. Tears of repentance, according to Saint Isaac, are the signs of the awakening of that inner man.

"I have known people," the staretz said, "who passed through this blessed valley of tears. Saint Isaac says truly that those who received the grace of tears find out that wandering thoughts during the time of prayer cease and their very nature is changed. Such contemplatives enter into the peace described in the Epistle to the Hebrews. When this peace is attained, their minds begin to contemplate the mysteries. The Holy Spirit begins to reveal to the mystic heavenly things. God comes to dwell in him."

Father Michael celebrated the Liturgy alone each day, just as Bishop Theophan the Recluse had done.

"Nothing," he said, "makes a priest better and more spiritual than the daily celebration of the Holy Liturgy. But we must remember the saying of one great mystic. No one should celebrate or take communion unless he does so with tears of repentance and joy." The staretz recommended frequent communion to the laity.

The discussion on the Divine will was most illuminating.

"Nothing happens in this world," Father Michael said to me, "apart from the will of God. By his will, for example, you left Russia for the West without knowing where you would go and why. God has settled you now in Oxford in England and you now write books and articles. Again by the will of God you came here to see me. Why? You do not know at present but you will understand in due course. The same thing happens to everybody, myself included."

The staretz told me then the story of his own ordination and also the story of a bishop.

The fourth talk was almost entirely devoted to mystical subjects. At that meeting Father Michael handed me another leaflet. It not only answered my question but summed up all our talks.

The leaflet was entitled: *Attain peace of mind*. On the last day of his life, the leaflet stated, Saint Seraphim of Sarov thrice said to a monk whom he loved: "Attain peace of mind, Father."

"What Saint Seraphim said to that monk I repeat to you. If we have no peace of mind, we cannot see God. We are able to understand Divine Providence looking to our past but we do not know what to do now and what to plan for the future. If we have no inner peace it means that we are still divided in ourselves and blinded with passions which prevent us from seeing the world as it really is. But when we attain inner peace our passions are mastered and we see clearly who we are and where we are going. It is impossible to be a good servant of the Lord and to labor in his vineyard in whatsoever capacity with any success unless inner peace is attained first. People value this peace above all else but it is obvious they cannot obtain it from those who do not have it themselves. So many sermons, books and exercises produce no effect because they are not born of inner peace, meditation and detachment. But when you attain inner peace everything is all right because God is with you. Only in deep inner peace can we see God and understand his will. All our works, however secure and solid they might appear, are built on shifting sands and will collapse, as the house on sand about which we read in the Gospel, unless we attain serenity of mind and know where to build and how to build."

Father Michael then gave me some personal counsels. His views on silence, with which we finished our conversation, were taken from Saint Isaac the Syrian:

> When you put on one side every ascetic exercise and on the other silence, you will soon find out that the latter is the most important of all. People give us many counsels but when we become familiar with silence all human counsels become superfluous as well as all our former works. We will find that they all belong to the past and that we approach perfection.

Father Michael obviously wanted to return to his solitude.

I attended on one occasion the Liturgy which he said alone during the night. This was a true Liturgy of contemplation. The notion of time and space melted away. This was eternity. How long this Liturgy lasted I cannot say. It seemed time stood still.

To describe the personality of Father Michael I would use a description given to us by Saint Macarius the Great, an Egyptian mystic of the fourth century, which I have found in the *Dobrotolyubie* of Bishop Theophan the Recluse. Saint Macarius writes of the true mystic:

> In him grace acts in such a way that his body and heart are in deep peace. His soul in its tremendous joy becomes like that of the innocent child. He judges no one, neither

Greek nor Jew, neither sinner nor layman. This inner man looks on everyone equally. He rejoices with the entire world. His only desire is to honor and to love the Greek and the Jew. He is the son of the King because he trusts in the Son of God as his father. The door of the invisible world opens before him and he enters into many mansions. And once he enters these mansions, the doors of others open before him. If he entered a hundred mansions, the doors of another hundred would open. He is continually enriched. The more he is enriched, the more are the wonders revealed to him. To him, as to the son and heir, God entrusts that which cannot be apprehended by human nature or expressed by word.

Such was Father Michael. This is the true portrait of the Russian mystic, beginning with Saint Sergius of Radonezh, Saint Nilus of Sora, Paissy Velichkovsky, Saint Seraphim of Sarov and many others and ending with Father Michael.

One of the mystics Father Michael loved very much was Saint Seraphim of Sarov (1759-1833), the first and greatest of the saints of the nineteenth century. Of all the saints of Russia he is perhaps the most immediately attractive to non-Orthodox Christians. Prokhor Moshnin, later named Seraphim, while still a very young man, entered the Sarov Monastery and performed his tasks with dedication and joy. The rule of his staretz, to pray always the Jesus Prayer, released a longing to live as a hermit. With the permission of his elders he lived alone in the forest for many years. One day three robbers wounded him badly. From then on he lived as a recluse in the monastery. He attained purity of heart and received the gift of seeing into people's souls. He was also blessed with several apparitions of the Mother of God. In 1813 he opened his cell and started to help people in spiritual need. The last twenty years of his life were full of activity. He founded a convent, gave encouragement to the many people who daily flocked to the door of his cell and healed the sick, welcoming them with the joyful Easter words, "Christ is risen, My Joy!" By his warning he also prepared the Russian Church to hold firm against the coming age of atheism.

Early in the morning on January 2, 1833, he was found dead kneeling before the Icon of Our Lady of Umilenie. The veneration of Seraphim as a saint immediately spread far and wide. In July, 1903, his solemn canonization was performed in Sarov. My grandmother, Maria Nikolaevna, was among those present. She told me, "I was at Sarov when Saint Seraphim was canonized and I saw his hermitage and the rock on which he prayed, one thousand days and one thousand nights. He was a great staretz because he always practiced the Jesus Prayer."

One day I was sitting with Father Michael in his cell. The day was declining toward evening and twilight filled the room. In the corner, before the icons, an oil lamp flickered. All was quiet and at peace. A holy light, in a spiritual silence, like the movement of angels' wings, reigned over the room.

"Tell me, Father Michael, what are the tears of grace?"

"The tears of grace, my friend, are the sign of perfect prayer and of the forgiveness of sins. Saint Isaac the Syrian writes well on this subject." Father Michael took a book from his table and handed it to me: "Read, please, the marked passages."

"Yes, Father Michael," I said. Taking the book, I started to read:

When your soul is approaching the time to leave its obscurity, this will be your sign. Your heart will begin to burn as fire and every day and night it will burn more strongly. The entire world becomes for you a cloud of dust and ashes. You do not even want to eat because of the sweet, new, fiery thoughts unceasingly awakening in your soul. Suddenly a source of tears is granted to you. It is a stream which runs on effortlessly and mixes with all your deeds, while you are reading, praying, meditating, eating, drinking, and so on. When you see this happening in your soul, be of good cheer because you have crossed the sea. Keep continuous watch in order to grow daily in grace. Until you experience this state, your journey is not yet finished; you have not yet ascended the mountain of God. If, after all this, you see your tears drying up and your fire dying down without bodily sickness, woe to you! You perished either by pride or by neglect and laziness.

As long as you have not yet entered the valley of tears, your inner man serves the world. This means you still lead a worldly life and work for God only outwardly; your inner man remains sterile because his fruitfulness begins with tears. When you do reach the valley of tears, you will know that your mind has left the prison of this world and has entered upon the path of a new time and has begun to smell the perfume of the wonderful new air. These tears begin to flow because the time of the birth of the spiritual child is near. Our common mother, Grace, wishes to produce in us in her own mysterious way the divine image so that we may see the light of the age to come. This phenomenon of tears is not the same as that which is experienced at times by solitaries, sometimes while they are contemplating, sometimes while reading or praying. I speak not of a passing experience but of tears that run unceasingly day and night, like a river, for two years or more. Perfect serenity of mind follows upon this. And with it, according to our measure, our mind enters into the state described by Saint Paul the Apostle. In that peace of mind one begins to contemplate Divine Mysteries. Then the Holy Spirit opens heaven to the contemplative.

God comes to dwell in him and resurrects in him the fruit of the Spirit. But listen further: once you enter into the region of the purification of your thoughts you lose the abundance of tears and they come only in a proper time and measure.

I stopped and looked at Father Michael. "I see that you have wept a great deal in your life, Father Michael."

"Yes, I have," the staretz answered simply.

"I do not know why, Father, but one book moves me much to tears whenever I read it, even when I am reading it in the British Museum in London."

"Is it a good book, Brother Sergius?"

"Yes, it contains a boy's reminiscences of his childhood in a pious Moscow family in the last years of the reign of Alexander II."

"Yes, my friend, in our age of unbelief and carnal life we have become cold. Tears are considered a manifestation of pitiful weakness, something to be despised, good, perhaps, for old women but no one else. On the other hand, a stony indifference and hardness of heart are regarded as virility, self-possession, *sang-froid*. But, in truth, such an absence of tenderheartedness is merely a sign of spiritual death. A Byzantine mystic once said that those who go to Holy Communion without tears and a tender heart and still more those who, celebrating the Holy Liturgy, remain stonily indifferent, all of them eat and drink the Body and the Blood of the Lord unworthily. They are subject to condemnation. Therefore, cultivate tears and tenderness of heart because only through them can we come to the purification of our thoughts. There is no other way."

"Tell me, Father Michael," I continued, "what can you say of the Light of Tabor? I have read several descriptions of that Light. For instance, in the fifth volume of *Dobrotolyubie* there is a description of that Light as seen by Saint Symeon the New Theologian. The experience is described in the third person, of course, according to the custom of the times. I copied the description, and here it is:

Once, when he stood up in prayer, saying more with his mind than with his lips: "God, have mercy on me, a sinner," he was suddenly illuminated from above with the resplendent Divine Light, which filled the room. At that moment the young man forgot that he was in the room and under the roof. He was surrounded by the Light on every side and he did not know whether he was still on earth or not. The young man then lost all earthly cares and anxieties. Nothing earthly or carnal came to his mind. He was all melted into this immaterial Light. It appeared to him that he himself became light. He forgot all that went on and was filled with an indescribable joy. Afterward his mind ascended to heaven and he contemplated there another Light, much brighter than that around him. And he saw in that shining Light the staretz who gave him the rule of prayer and the treatise of Saint Mark the Ascetic."

"In the life of Saint Symeon," Father Michael answered, "this vision appeared in the very beginning of his conversion. The Light of Tabor is the grace of God, given to those whom he wills. So it is also with the tears of grace. They are unobtainable by any effort of ours. The vision of Divine Light filled Symeon with tears. The Lord gives this Light as sign and promise, either to urge a man to go the right way or to retain him in it."

"I read of similar visions," I continued, "in the life of Saint Tikhon of Zadonsk, Abbot Anthony Putilov of Maloyaroslavetz and the Megaloschemos Ignaty, restorer of Zadne-Nikiforovsky Pustin in the province of Olonets, who died in 1849 at the age of seventy. Father Ignaty writes:

Once, when I was sitting in my cell meditating and tears were streaming from my eyes, I fell into something like an ecstasy. My soul contemplated the immaterial Light and I saw myself as made of light and my body dead, abandoned by the soul.

"Dr. Rozov told me of a similar experience he had when in Pskovo-Petchersky Monastery in 1926. I discussed various spiritual phenomena with the Doctor."

130

"If you have experienced something similar or do sometime in the future, meditate much on the conversation between Saint Seraphim of Sarov and Motovilov. This conversation, described by Motovilov, was published by Nilus shortly before the First World War. I have the first edition of this remarkable Motovilov manuscript. Take it and read aloud the marked passages and I will comment on them."

I took the booklet from Father Michael and began reading the words of Saint Seraphim to Motovilov:

> Prayer, fasting, vigils and all other Christian deeds, however good they may be in themselves, are, nevertheless, not the purpose of Christian life although they are needed to attain it. The true purpose of Christian life consists in acquiring the Holy Spirit of God. Note, Father, that only deeds performed for Christ's sake bring us the fruits of the Holy Spirit. Anything that is not performed for Christ's sake, howsoever good in itself, does not bring us a reward in the future life.
>
> For this reason the Lord Jesus Christ said: Everyone who does not gather with me, scatters. The acquisition of this Spirit of God is the true goal of our Christian life, while prayer, fasting, alms and all the other virtues for Christ's sake are merely means toward the first. Indeed, every good work for Christ's sake earns for us the grace of the Holy Spirit but prayer gives the most because it is always at our disposal as a means to acquire the grace of the Spirit.
>
> With all other virtues for Christ's sake it is not the same. Either we lack the strength of character, for instance to preserve virginity, or we have no opportunity, as with almsgiving. It is different with prayer. Everyone may use it everywhere, wealthy and poor, nobleman and commoner, strong and weak, healthy and sick, just and sinner. Great is the power of prayer and it is suitable for

everyone. By prayer we are honored to talk with our all-good God and Savior. Yet there is only so much we can do, till the Holy Spirit overshadows us, in the measure of his heavenly grace known to him alone. When by his good will he visits us, we must cease to pray. Why pray then: Come, Holy Spirit, when he has already come to us in order to save those who trust in him and invoke his Holy Name?

"Father Michael," I said, interrupting the reading, "this passage is not quite clear to me. Is it true that when the Holy Spirit descends upon us, our prayer stops?"

"Yes," he said, "that is true. All the mystics have taught this. Prayer exists whenever we make an effort to say it in whatever form but when the Holy Spirit overshadows us no effort is needed and our prayer ceases. When the Holy Spirit descends upon us, we remain continually in prayerful sentiments towards God without words and without images. This is unceasing prayer. Now continue your reading."

If, for instance, Divine Grace grants you prayer and watchfulness over your thoughts, pray and watch. If Divine Grace gives you the ability to fast with profit, do so. If you are attracted to works of charity, this is your way. Judge likewise of every good deed done for Christ's sake.

"You see, Brother Sergius," Father Michael interjected, "everyone has his own vocation from the Lord. One is attracted to the solitary life, another to fasting, a third to almsgiving, a fourth to virginity, et cetera. Whatever approach brings you nearer to God, do. Father John of Kronstadt had one vocation, while Bishop Theophan the Recluse had another. The first was a preacher and the second a writer. The first was continually with people, while the second received no one. And yet both were holy men. Go by your own way without judging other people or which way is best. The Savior forbade his disciples to do this."

I continued reading:

We in our time, because of our general indifference to our holy faith in our Lord Jesus Christ and our lack of attention to his Divine Providence for us, have reached such a degree of indifference, we may say, that we have abandoned true Christian life altogether. We now consider strange the words of Sacred Scripture where the Holy Spirit says by Moses: "And I then saw the Lord walking in paradise" or when we read in the Epistle of Saint Paul the Apostle: "We went to Achaia and the Spirit of God did not walk with us and when we returned to Macedonia, the Spirit of God was with us." In many other places of Sacred Scripture we read of Divine manifestations to men. "Well," some people say, "those passages are hard to understand; how could those men see God?" And yet this is quite understandable. This misunderstanding came about because we gave up the simplicity of the original Christian vision and under the pretext of higher education became so ignorant that we consider hardly possible things that the ancients understand clearly. The mention of God's manifestation in ordinary conversation did not seem strange to them.

"All this is perfectly clear," Father Michael observed, "to anyone who leads a life of prayer. Divine Providence is always with us. If we labor for Christ, like the Apostle Paul, the Holy Spirit favors us but if we fall into our own agitated ways he leaves us. Generally speaking, works for God's sake progress easily albeit with some obstacles in order to prove us. On the contrary, if obstacles grow all the time in spite of our best efforts, it is a sign that the Spirit of God is not with us and we should give up our undertaking. Read on, please."

Men saw God and the grace of the Holy Spirit neither in sleep nor in daydreaming, nor in disturbed, sickly imagination but in truth, in reality. When our Lord Jesus Christ had completed the work of salvation, after his Resurrection, he breathed upon the Apostles, renewing the breath of life lost by Adam, and gave us the same Adam's Grace of the All Holy Spirit of God. On the day of Pentecost he sent the Holy Spirit to the Apostles in a mighty wind in the form of fiery tongues. This very fire-like Grace of the Holy Spirit, given to us in the mystery of Holy Baptism, is sealed on the principal spots of our flesh as an eternal tabernacle of this Grace. The priest then says: "The Seal of the Gift of the Holy Spirit...." If we did not sin after our baptism, we would remain forever holy and sinless, free from all impurity of the flesh and spirit, saints of God.

The trouble is that as we advance in years, we do not advance in Grace and the Mind of God, as did our Lord Jesus Christ but, on the contrary, by befouling ourselves, little by little we lose Divine Grace and become in various degrees sinful and even very sinful people.

Still, if we, being awakened by Divine Wisdom, which seeks our salvation, decided for its sake to pray and watch over ourselves to attain eternal salvation, we must, obedient to its voice, repent truly of all our sins and acquire the virtues opposed to them and thereby gain the Holy Spirit who acts within us and builds there the Kingdom of God. The Grace of the Holy Spirit, given in baptism in the Name of the Father and of the Son and of the Holy Spirit, in spite of the darkness surrounding our soul, nevertheless shines always with the light of the priceless merits of Christ. This light of Christ converts sinners to the way of penance, removing every trace of committed crimes and clothes the former criminal once more with incorruptible clothing, the Grace of the Holy Spirit, to acquire

134

which is the purpose of the Christian life, as I have already told you.

The Grace of the Holy Spirit is the Light that illumines us. Many times, before many witnesses, the active Grace of the Holy Spirit has manifested itself around those people whom he illumined by his descent. Remember Moses after his colloquy with God on the mountain of Sinai. People could not look on his face as he was shining with the unusual light surrounding him. For that reason he was obliged to appear before the people with his face veiled. Remember also the Transfiguration of the Lord on Mount Tabor: "And his clothes shone like snow and his disciples prostrated themselves in fear." When Elijah and Moses appeared, the cloud overshadowed the disciples, too, in order to hide from them the Light of Divine Grace. In this way the Grace of the All-Holy Spirit of God appears in indescribable light to all to whom God manifests it.

Everything is simple to the wise man. Being in this mind, the Apostles always knew whether the Spirit of God was with them or not. Penetrated by him and seeing the presence within themselves of the Divine Spirit, they recognized that their labor was holy and well pleasing to God. They wrote in their Epistles: "According to the Holy Spirit's decision and our own." And only on that basis did they propose their Epistles as unchanging truth for the benefit of all believers.

"Now, my friend," Father Michael said, "read the description of the descent of the Holy Spirit witnessed by Motovilov. I will comment in due course."

I resumed my reading with Saint Seraphim speaking to Motovilov:

"Why do you not look at me?" Motovilov answered: "I cannot look at you, Father, because lightning streams from your eyes, and my eyes ache." Father Seraphim said: "Do not be afraid, Lover of God, because you are now as shining as myself. You are now in the fullness of the Spirit of God, because otherwise you could not see me in that state!" And inclining his head he said, whispering into my ear: "Thanks be to God for his indescribable mercy to you. You see, I did not even cross myself but merely prayed to God mentally in my heart and said: 'Lord, make him worthy to see clearly with his bodily eyes the descent of your Holy Spirit as you do when you manifest yourself in the light of your magnificent glory.' And you see, the Lord accomplished at once the humble request of his unworthy Seraphim. Now we should thank him for this indescribable gift to both of us. The Lord rarely manifests himself in this way even to great ascetics. May this Divine Grace console your distressed heart as a loving mother does her children on the request of the Mother of God herself. Why do you still not look into my eyes? Look simply and do not fear. The Lord is with us."

After these words I looked at his face and an even greater and more respectful fear seized me. Picture to yourself the face of the man who speaks to you in the middle of the sun at its noonday brightest. You see the movements of his lips and the changing expressions of his face. You hear his voice and you feel that he keeps his hands on your shoulder but you see neither his hands nor yourself nor him but only the blinding light extending many yards in every direction, illuminating with a brilliant glow the snowy mantle of the meadow and the snow falling from above on myself and the great staretz. Is it possible to picture my state then?

"How do you feel now?" the staretz asked me.

"Exceptionally well," I replied.

"But how well? What particularly?"

"I feel an inexpressible stillness and peace in my soul."

"This, Lover of God," said Father Seraphim, "is that peace of which the Lord said to his disciples: 'I give you my peace; not as the world gives do I give you. If you were of the world, the world would love its own. But as I have chosen you from the world, the world hates you. But be of good cheer, because I have overcome the world.' To people hated by the world but chosen by the Lord he gives that peace which you now feel within you. 'A peace,' according to the word of the Apostle, 'transcending all reason.'"

"Do you see," Father Michael intervened, "the Light seen by Motovilov, Symeon the New Theologian, Schimonk Germanus, Saint Tikhon of Zadonsk and others is the same as that which the Apostles contemplated when the Lord underwent transfiguration on Mount Tabor in order for them to see even in their lifetime that Kingdom of God come in power? Observe, too, that the Lord did not take all the Apostles up the mount but only three of them. And yet all of these three abandoned him and the Apostle Peter thrice denied him. Saint Symeon the New Theologian saw this Light when he was still a young man and soon afterward returned to a worldly life. Motovilov was the pious owner of a country estate and that was all. Yet he contemplated the Light of Tabor. The grace to see this Light is given only to those to whom it is needful, either to console them, as in the case of Motovilov, or to strengthen them, as with the Apostles. Read on, dear Sergius."

I continued my reading of the notes of Motovilov:

"What do you feel more?"

"The exceptional joy of my heart."

And Father Seraphim continued: "When the Spirit of

God descends on us and overshadows us with his Grace, our soul overflows with an inexplicable joy because the Holy Spirit makes everything joyful when he touches it. It is the same joy about which the Lord speaks in the Gospel: 'A woman, while she is in travail, endures sorrow because her hour has come; but when she has delivered her child, she forgets her sorrow for joy because a man has been born into the world. In the world you will be sorrowful, but when I shall visit you, you will be joyful and no one can take away your joy.' However, the joy felt by you now is consoling to your heart. It is nothing compared with that joy of which the Lord himself spoke through his Apostle: 'Neither eye has seen nor ear heard nor the heart conceived the well-being which God has prepared for those who love him.'

"If the beginnings of this joy which are given to us now make us so well and happy in our souls, what shall we say of that joy which is prepared in heaven for those who weep here on earth? You, little father, wept enough in your lifetime and see with what joy the Lord consoled you even in this earthly life.

"What more do you feel, Lover of God?"

I answered: "An extraordinary warmth."

"What kind of warmth, little father? We are sitting in the forest. It is winter, there is snow above us and beneath us. What warmth could there be in such conditions?"

I answered: "Such warmth as there is in the Russian bath when water is poured on the heated stones and the steam rises in a column."

"And is the smell the same as in the bath?" he asked me.

"No," I replied, "there is no such perfume on earth. When my mother was still living I greatly loved to dance and used to go to dances and balls in the evening. My mother used to sprinkle me with perfumes which she purchased in the best and most fashionable shops in Kazan but those perfumes were never as pleasing as these."

Father Seraphim, smiling pleasantly, said to me: "I know that as well as you do, but I asked you for a purpose whether you felt this way. It is perfectly true, Lover of God, no pleasant earthly perfume can be compared with that which we sense now because we are surrounded with the perfume of the Holy Spirit of God.

"You said that around us it is as warm as in the Russian bath but look, neither on me nor on you does the snow melt nor above us either. It means that this warmth is not in the atmosphere but within ourselves. It is the same warmth for which the Holy Spirit makes us cry out in the words of the prayer: 'Warm me with the heat of the Holy Spirit.' Because of this, hermits — men and women — did not fear the winter's cold, being clothed, as in warmest furs, in the vestments of grace made by the Holy Spirit. This must be so because the Grace of God must dwell within us, in our heart.

"The Lord said, 'The Kingdom of God is within you.' By this Kingdom of God the Lord means the Grace of the Holy Spirit. Well, this same Kingdom of God is now within us while the Grace of the Holy Spirit shines and warms us, filling the air around us with various perfumes and sweetens our organs of sensation with heavenly pleasure and our hearts with indescribable joy. Our present state is the same as that about which the Apostle says: 'The Kingdom of God is neither food nor drink, but truth and peace in the Holy Spirit.' Our holy faith does not consist of persuasive words of human wisdom, but in the manifestation of spirit and strength. We are now in that very state of which the Lord said: 'There are some among those present who will see the Kingdom of God come in strength before they taste death.' Well, little father, Lover of God, you understand with what indescribable joy the Lord God has rewarded us. This is what it means to be in the fullness of the Holy Spirit of which Saint Macarius of Egypt says: 'I was myself in the fullness of the Holy Spirit. Now the Lord filled my unworthiness with the fullness of the Holy Spirit.'"

I stopped reading.

Father Michael sat in his chair, meditatively, with his prayer cord in his hand. "Did you understand, dear Sergius, the significance of this speech?"

"Yes, I understand now that the Light of Tabor is the shining of the Holy Spirit when he descends upon us; it bespeaks the fullness of the Holy Spirit."

"Good. Now continue reading the marked passages."

I continued reading:

"Little father, you are a layman and I am a monk, but it is of no importance. God sees true faith in himself and in his only-begotten Son. For that he gives richly from above the Grace of the Holy Spirit. The Lord is searching for the heart that is filled with love for God and for neighbor. This is the throne upon which he loves to sit in the fullness of his heavenly glory. The Lord listens equally to a monk and to a layman, a simple Christian, if they are both Orthodox and love God from the depth of their soul. If they have faith in him, even as small as a mustard seed, they will both move mountains.

"The Lord himself says that everything is possible to him who believes, while Saint Paul the Apostle says: 'I can do all things in Christ, who strengthens me.' Therefore have no doubt that the Lord God will answer your request if it is made for the glory of God and for the edification of your neighbors. And even if your request is for your own needs or benefit, if they are necessary to you the Lord God will grant you all you ask for, because the Lord loves those who love him and will hear them and grant their requests."

"You see, dear Sergius," Father Michael observed, "how needful faith is. Without it, according to the Apostle, we cannot please God because we must believe that he exists and rewards those who love him. Otherwise prayer is impossible. Again, our faith must be strong, free of doubts, because men of double heart will not be accepted. You wanted to know what the Light of Tabor is? Well, Saint Seraphim explains the matter very clearly. There is nothing to add."

My last conversation with Father Michael was the deepest and the most instructive. Father Michael was over eighty then but his heart and mind were young. I sat in his cell. It was a warm evening in August. The sun was setting on the other side of the lake, behind the endless forests. The deep silence reminded me of Levitan's picture *Eternal Rest*.

"Tell me, Father Michael, what are the main stages in the spiritual life?"

"They are just as Father Arkadi explained to you at the Pskovo-Petchersky Monastery in Estonia. No one can ever be saved without humility. Remember, to the end of your days you will fall into sins, major and minor ones. You will be quick-tempered, vain, untruthful, avaricious, tyrannical. The knowledge of this should make you humble. How can you become proud when you know very well that you sin daily and hurt your neighbor? Yet for every sin there is repentance. If you have sinned, repent; if you have sinned again, repent again and so until the end. Doing this, you will never despair but will gradually achieve a peaceful soul. But to achieve this, you must guard your thoughts. They can be good or evil. The evil ones you should never accept. As soon as a temptation turns up, cut it down at once with the Jesus Prayer as with a sword. But if you start to analyze it, it will attract your attention, maybe interest you; it will overcome you, you will agree to it and will begin to think how to carry it out and there, the sin has been committed. There are also thoughts that seem innocent but can lead to great temptations and grave sins. I was told that in a convent in the Urals, there was a spiritual nun and the priest of that convent, a very good priest, was a widower, about sixty years of age. One evening, going to bed, he suddenly remembered how, thirty years before, when his wife was alive, he used to help her put the children to bed and was moved by emotion. Then he remembered his wife and his life with her and so it went. His thoughts began to roam where they shouldn't. Terrified he spent the entire night in prayers and prostrations. In the morning the old nun called him to her and said: 'Into what temptation did you fall, Father? I saw the evil powers encircling you like flies.' The Father contritely admitted his sin. This is where our thoughts can lead us, even if at first they seem innocent. Psychiatrists speak to us of psychoanalysis and other things, but without their science we can know bad from good. For this reason, it is best to call out to God without ceasing: 'Lord Jesus Christ, Son of God, have mercy on me, a sinner.' The Apostle Paul says: 'The one who confesses Christ as the Son of God and cries out to him without ceasing, will be saved.'

"You, Sereyenka, practice as much as you can the Jesus Prayer and gradually you will acquire peace and a sign of this will be for you a deep peace within the soul, an almost continual silence."

"And what happens then, Father Michael?" I asked the staretz.

"This is what happens. There are two forms of silence. The first is the ordinary external silence. This form is not bad. Here at least one does not tempt or wrong others. Yet this is not enough. The Desert Fathers said that an ascetic sitting alone in his cave is like an asp in its nest full of deadly poison if he remembers wrongs inflicted upon him at some time in the past and brews his anger. The second form of silence is inner silence. The same Fathers spoke of it in this way: There are elders who speak from morning until night yet remain silent all the while. For they do not say anything that is not beneficial for others or for themselves. This is inner silence. Try to attain it, Sereyenka. And when you attain it and cease to judge others then arise and give thanks to the Lord who has granted you such a great mercy. Then you will not be far from purity of heart and you know that only the pure of heart can see God.

"Others, however, have a different path to travel, the path of grace-filled tears. These tears are not those which one has when losing a close one or reading a book or hearing a sermon. Grace-filled tears pour forth as streams. They flow two years or more without ceasing. They burn all impurities in us. Then the soul becomes peaceful and sees God."

"What does it mean, Father Michael, 'to see God'? Is this a metaphor or something else?"

Father Michael looked at me inquisitively and contemplated my question. "Of course: 'No one has seen God at any time. The Son, who is in the bosom of the Father, he has declared him.' It is also said: 'The Cherubim and Seraphim, which go before him, cover their faces.' Not only are we unable to see God but the essence of God we will never comprehend. Yet we are able to see God's glory, the uncreated and incomprehensible Light of Tabor which was seen by the three elect Apostles on the Mount. This is the Light which Motovilov saw when he spoke to Saint Seraphim. This is the descent of the Holy Spirit, the Kingdom of God which is come in power. Such a thing was seen by the holy Tikhon of Zadonsk before he became a bishop. As a youth, the future Abbot Anthony Putilov of Maloyaroslav was also found worthy to see it. I won't even speak of the visions of Saint Symeon the New Theologian. Very few see this sight, only God's elect."

"Tell me, Father, are there ascetics now living who have seen this Light of Tabor?"

"And why not? We must assume that such strugglers exist. But why ask about this? Since you believe that this Light appears, why

143

must you know more? Blessed are they that have not seen and yet have believed. Motovilov was allowed to see this Light as an *ouverenie*, a 'sign.'"

"What is meant by *ouverenie*, Father Michael?"

"Well, here it is. In the account of the life of Staretz Daniel of Achinsk, a Siberian ascetic, highly respected by Saint Seraphim, the following incident is recorded. A wealthy Siberian woman, a spiritual daughter of Staretz Daniel, decided to enter a convent. She visited a number of women's communities in Russia and Siberia and could not decide which to choose. She went to Father Daniel and asked him to direct her to the right one.

"He answered her: 'If I tell you which one and you are not happy there, you will say later: "I would never have entered this convent if it weren't for the staretz." You will be angry with me and dissatisfied with yourself. Continue to seek and when you find the right one, your heart will be filled with joy and that will be for you as an *ouverenie*.' And so it happened that the Siberian woman visited the convent at Irkutsk. Her heart filled with joy, she remained there and later became the Abbess Susanna.

"Your mission, Sereyenka, is the same as the one described by Saint Seraphim to Father Timon, the Abbot of Nadeevsk:

> Sow the good seed wherever it may land: by the wayside, among thorns, on stony places, on good ground. Some seeds will sprout and bring forth fruit, even a hundred-fold.

"One must always try to attain peace of soul, for no good can come out of a soul torn by passions and sin. When you finally settle down and become wise you will be able to accomplish much. I spoke to you of inner silence. That is true seclusion, the real life of a hermit, while the Jesus Prayer is the Divine Service, performed ceaselessly in the temple of your heart, where also lies the Kingdom of God."

144

On August 16, the very day of my departure from Uusi Valamo, I attended the Liturgy celebrated by Father Michael in his hermitage and took Holy Communion from him. Father Michael said the Liturgy alone in his private chapel. After breakfast I took my leave of Father.

I met Father Michael once more in Pskovo-Petchersky Monastery in July, 1960. Blessing me at that time, Father Michael said as his farewell: "Continue your efforts. Keep contact with Father Ilian on Mount Athos and the Lord will be with you."

About two years later, Father Michael died. He was buried with great solemnity and now rests in the catacombs of the monastery.

Part IV

Mount Athos

In his well-known book *Russian Mystics* Serge Bolshakoff writes: "There are, in fact, three Mount Athos: The first, the Mount Athos of tourists, is described in many books and articles in dozens of languages. The second, the Mount Athos of scholars and artists, is also well-known and there are a great many learned studies on the history, sociology, art and literature of the Mount. The third, the Mount Athos of mystics, is very little known and well-nigh impenetrable." For Serge it was definitely the third Mount Athos for which he searched.

About mystics he writes: "I consider mystics those people who have reached union with God through unceasing prayer of the heart, custody of the thoughts and complete surrender to the Divine will." He also wrote: "...true mystics are rare, exceedingly rare.... They avoid publicity as a plague and do not reveal themselves to everybody, but only to those who, according to their judgment, are apt to benefit from their sayings."

Serge Bolshakoff visited Mount Athos twice, in 1954 and 1957, and on both occasions he stayed at the Russian Monastery of Saint Panteleimon. There he met Father Ilian who "...was the last representative of the long line of Saint Panteleimon's mystics and ascetics." Serge had many talks with this father which he committed to paper several times.

On the recommendation of Father Ilian, Serge also visited the Greek Monastery of Dionysiou at Mount Athos in 1954 to make the acquaintance of Father Euthemios, who was called a *yurodivini*, a Fool for Christ's sake.

CHAPTER 19

Father Ilian

I came to Saint Panteleimon's, the Russian monastery on Mount Athos, in November, 1954, one sunny evening. It had been a long day's journey from Thessaloniki in northern Greece. On the second day after my arrival I met Father Ilian, then confessor of the community. In time he would become the hegumen or abbot. He was an old monk of great dignity with the spirit shinning in his face. He looked like one of the holy old Fathers of the Desert as they appeared in the icons.

Our first conversation was remarkable and reminded me of my first meeting with Father Michael, the recluse of Uusi Valamo.

"You know, Sergei Nikolaevitch," Father Ilian said to me, "nothing happens in this world, created by God, without his will. You came here, sent by Divine Providence. You don't know now, probably, why you did come here but you will realize this later on. Something like this happened to myself. Born in 1883 in the province of Yaroslav in Russia, I belonged to a well-off merchant family. We had a flourishing business in Saint Petersburg. I had before me the prospects of a fine business career. Yet I wasn't attracted to it but rather to monastic life. I asked my parents to allow me to follow my vocation. They agreed. I began to visit monasteries, going first to Valaam on the Archipelago in the Lake of Ladoga. It was a great monastery with many saintly monks but I felt it was not my place. In 1902 I entered as a novice the Glinskaya Pustin, well known for its startzy. I expected to remain there for life. However, my staretz told me one day: 'John, your place isn't here but on Athos. Go to Saint Panteleimon's and you will find there peace for your soul.' I was rather astonished with this order but obeyed and in 1905 I came here. I learned soon that this monastery was my place. In 1908 I was professed with the name of Ilian, one of the martyrs of Sebaste in Armenia. This name means sunny or radiant. All my life I tried therefore to realize the name of my patron in deed by being radiant under all circumstances. Our name should have a meaning for us. We should be joyful. Saint Paul exhorts us: 'Be joyful always.'"

"When I visited Staretz Michael in Uusi Valamo," I answered, "he told me Saint Seraphim of Sarov greeted his visitors with the words: 'My joy.' He also advised people to attain serenity of soul which will help many people to be saved. Is it true?"

"Certainly. Once we attain peace of soul we shall be radiant and attract people to us. People in this world are, generally speaking, unhappy and uneasy. They look always, even without realizing it, for those who can procure joy for them — not passing pleasure, but abiding joy."

"Father Michael said something similar to that to me in Uusi Valamo," I added. I then told him my story.

Father Ilian listened to me with attention and said: "Leave all that to God and he will direct you. Do you practice the Jesus Prayer?"

"Yes, I do."

"Then everything is all right. Do as you were instructed. Gradually your prayer will become continuous. You will pray then while walking, working, even sleeping, according to the saying: 'I sleep but my heart watches.' Your life becomes prayer.

"When a person arrives at this degree of the prayer of the heart he is transformed, always patient, humble, faithful and serene. Under the greatest provocation he remains quiet. He sleeps well, even if he sleeps little. He is always in a good mood. He has nothing but is master of everything."

150

"I suppose, Father, such a prayer is reserved only for contemplative monks."

"It is easier for them to attain it but it is possible for everybody, even for those living in the world. No place can save us. We must do this work ourselves. Satan was a leading angel and yet perished. Among the twelve Apostles there was a traitor."

During my first stay in Saint Panteleimon, in 1954, I met Father Ilian rarely and we had little opportunity to talk together.

When I visited Mount Athos once more, in the spring of 1957, Father Ilian was presiding over the monastery on behalf of the sick hegumen, Archimandrite Justin. During that stay I met Father Ilian nearly every day and had many talks with him. He used to come to the big, bright room that had been given to me in the old guest house above the gate of the monastery. Most of this building was to burn down in 1968. In the course of its history it had sheltered many distinguished pilgrims, including members of the Russian Imperial family.

Fine engravings of Saint Petersburg as well as portraits of Emperor Alexander III and of his wife, Empress Mary, and of the Metropolitan of Moscow, Filaret Drogoov, decorated the walls of my room. Two large windows looked out into the court of the monastery. The doors of my room opened onto a long veranda where the blue wisteria was in full bloom. From the veranda one could see the sea far below.

It was a marvelous Mount Athos spring with a blue cloudless sky, warm sunshine, limpid sea, plenty of flowers and the mighty snow peak of Mount Athos shining over all. It was the end of Easter week. The pure, warm air was filled with the perfume of the flowers.

I had many remarkable talks with Father Ilian. On one occasion he said to me:

"In order to have a long and useful life we must always rejoice in the Lord and have a serene and joyful spirit within ourselves. Never fall into sadness and depression as so many people do now. Practice the Jesus Prayer and it will lead you to this state. Of course you should also have a firm belief in Divine Providence and a pure conscience. Remember always the words of the Lord: 'Seek first the Kingdom of God and his righteousness and all things shall be added unto you.'"

On an April morning that was sunny and peaceful there was a knock at the door. Father Ilian entered my cell carrying with him a stack of books from the library for me to read.

"I have been reading, Father Ilian," I said, "the story of the journeys, across Russia, Moldavia, Turkey and the Holy Land, of Father Parfeny, a monk of Mount Athos. Do you know this book?"

"Yes, of course. I read it. That Father Parfeny, an Old Ritualist, was professed here and he was a friend and spiritual brother to our celebrated confessor of those days, Hieroschimonk Jerome Solomentsev. Father Parfeny's staretz, Father Arseny, sent him later to Siberia. Father Parfeny became hegumen of the Monastery of Guglitzi, near Moscow, and visited the Holy Mountain once more before his death."

"I have copied some things for myself from that book, Father Ilian, because I find them very wise. Listen, for instance, to this instruction which Schimonk John, a hermit of Vorona in Rumania, gave to Father Parfeny:

When you reach the Holy Mountain, choose for yourself an experienced staretz, father and instructor. Commit to him your body and soul and be obedient to him unto death. Live where he sends you to live. The Athonite startzy are superior to the Moldavian. I would like myself to live with them and to learn all that is needful. Indeed, I went twice to the Holy Mountain but the will of God and troubled times prevented me from remaining there for good and I returned to my Moldavian monastery.

Concerning future beatitude and how it can be attained, I shall tell you briefly. Wherever you live, wherever you wander, everywhere and in each place, the power of the

152

Lord and his mercy are present. You should live, of course, according to his will. No place sanctifies the man but the man sanctifies the place.

The will of God consists of the three principal virtues: faith, love, and hope. Faith comes first. It is the beginning of all the virtues. Without faith all good works are dead. The just man lives by faith. This faith is carried by fasting and is strengthened by prayer. Faith is perfected by obedience and the destruction of our self-will. In this way, it is acquired and matures. If you are unable to acquire such faith, you cannot acquire either trust in God or love for God and neighbor. If you fail to acquire them and are unable to purify the inner man, you cannot overcome passions.

Wherever you live, do not put your hope on any mortal, neither the Emperor nor the Prince, neither in the Patriarch nor the Bishop, not in merchants, nor in any man because every man is a liar. Do not trust in wealth, in the glory of this world, in your rank. Wealth is like the morning dew. Trust God alone. We must love the Lord God in such a way that we prefer nothing to him, especially not ourselves. The love of God is proved by our love of our neighbor. Our salvation consists in the sacrifice of ourselves and in watching over our hearts and in the unceasing Prayer of Jesus."

"Father Parfeny is right," observed Father Ilian. "People used to come to the Holy Mountain in search of spiritual direction. Once a staretz is found, he should be obeyed. Wherever he sends his disciple, the disciple must go. We must live in accord with the Divine will, that is, according to the commandments of Sacred Scripture, Church regulations and the instruction of the staretz. We must not rely on men, even the very best and just. Man is a flower. He blooms today and tomorrow he is no more. Father John, hegumen of

Petchenga, was right when he told you that once you have acquired spiritual wisdom you should be staretz to yourself because startzy are mortal, like everyone else. This was true of Father Parfeny. He was the disciple of a very great staretz, Hieroschimonk Arseny, who guided the Russian monks on the Holy Mountain at that time. But once Father Arseny died, Father Parfeny became his own staretz."

"Do you know, Father Ilian, that while in New Valamo, I often used to discuss with Father John the teaching of the startzy of Valaam on the Prayer of Jesus and its fruits. Father Parfeny describes the institution of the staretz itself very well. He came to Staretz Arseny and told him that he had chosen him to be his staretz and would obey his direction as to where to live and what to do. Father Arseny answered Father Parfeny in this way:

> You propose to make a great promise. If you persevere in it to the end, you will do well. Only, you must prepare yourself diligently to practice patience and to bear many sorrows and temptations. I will direct you, not according to your taste or your desire, neither according to my own human inclinations but according to the will of God. The Lord God does not want us, his servants, to live in bodily comfort, carnal pleasures and material well-being. He leads his faithful servants by a hard, narrow and sorrowful road. You see now, my dear brother, what is the way of Christ. To this world, the way of Christ is very sorrowful indeed. But if it is hard, it nonetheless leads to eternal beatitude while the broad and comfortable way leads to perdition. I will lead you by the narrow and hard way, according to the will of God although this way may appear to you cruel and insupportable. Will you go by this way to the end? It is easy to begin but the reward is given only to those who go on to the end. You came to the Holy Mountain with the intention of remaining here for life but it might happen that it will be necessary to send

you away to a place of which you have heard nothing. Such a mission might appear to you intolerable and you might refuse it. Therefore, do not promise to obey me but look first for some other staretz and confessor. There are many startzy on the Holy Mountain besides me. They live well and achieve their salvation.

"And it is true, Father Ilian. When Father Parfeny was professed and started to live on Mount Athos as a hermit, his heart was content. But Staretz Arseny ordered him to leave for Siberia, to a town entirely unknown to him. After some resistance Parfeny submitted to his staretz's order. He suffered much in Siberia before Metropolitan Filaret of Moscow, whose portrait is here, took an interest in him and changed his lot. In the end Father Parfeny became the founder and first hegumen of Guglitzi. What do you say of all this, Father Ilian?"

"I will tell you one thing only, my friend: The ways of Divine Providence are incomprehensible to us. Very often things that appear to us desirable and useful are not so in fact while things we detest are really needful for our salvation. Father Parfeny was a pilgrim for many years and he hoped to live quietly on the Holy Mountain and be consoled for his sorrows. In fact, he looked for some kind of rest and comfort. Well, Father Arseny saw through him and sent him to Siberia to worse trials until Parfeny realized his state and surrendered himself entirely to the Will of God. It is a fact that we serve very often our own desires and comfort while we imagine ourselves leading a holy life and going by the right way. While we are in reality advancing fast on the road to perdition we believe ourselves to be all right. No one is a good judge in his own case. This is why a staretz is so useful.

"We need to be patient, in no wise precipitous. If our business is from God it will right itself in the end but if it is merely our own illusion all our efforts will come to nought. Surrender to the Lord your way and he will perfect it. We need great spiritual experience to be able to select a correct way, especially in very complicated situations. As you know, I am a native of the province of Yaroslav, from Rostov. My childhood and early youth I spent in Saint Petersburg. I visited Valaam but I did not enter that community. I entered the Desert of Glinsky where I spent three years. But I did not remain there to make my profession. I came here to Saint Panteleimon's and here I have stayed. In 1932 I was sent to Siberia but I did not remain there as Archimandrite Parfeny did but returned here. The Lord led me by a way pleasing to him even though it has often been sorrowful for me for many reasons. Remember always: if your way of life is hard and sorrowful, it is correct but if you live in comfort, wealth and honor and still more, in carnal pleasures, you are on the broad way to perdition. It is quite impossible to attain serenity of mind without enduring many sorrows and for many years. We dislike sorrows although they benefit us. And we are attached fiercely to the comfort and pleasures that destroy us spiritually and bodily."

I went on, "I also love very much the following passage from the counsel of Father John of Vorona to Parfeny:

When I came to the Monastery of Neamtu and heard from Father Paissy how to begin and how to continue the Prayer of Jesus, I started to practice it. This Prayer appeared to me so sweet that I preferred it to everything else. For that reason I avoided other monks, loved silence, used often to retire to solitude, ran away from all temptations and most of all, idle talk. For the sake of the Prayer, I traveled twice to the Holy Mountain, fatigued myself with obedience and hard labor, metanias and all-night vigils in order to attain unceasing prayer. For the sake of the Prayer I often used to stay in solitude. In order to obtain it, I used up all my strength and became very weak. I continued in this way for many years and gradually the Prayer began to deepen. Afterwards, when I lived in the Skete of Pokrov, the Lord visited me because of the prayer of

Father Platon. Indescribable joy overshadowed my heart and the Prayer started to run by itself. It is so sweet now that it does not allow me to sleep. I sleep only one hour in twenty-four and that sitting up. And I rise up again as if I never slept. For even while I sleep my heart watches.

And the Prayer started to produce its fruits. It is true, the Kingdom of God is within us. There was born within me a love for everybody, something indescribable, and tears. I want to weep unceasingly. The Scripture of God, particularly the Gospels and the Psalms, became to me so sweet that I cannot enjoy them enough. Every word astonishes me and makes me cry much. O God, you manifested to me your unknowable and mysterious wisdom.

Often in the evening I rise up to read the Psalms or enter into the Prayer of Jesus and I experience ecstasy. I go out of myself, whether in the body or out of the body, and to whatever place I do not know. God knows. When I come to myself the sun is rising.

But temptations of the flesh besiege me to torment me in order to keep me humble. I cannot live with people, especially with lay folk. I cannot even talk to women. More than forty years passed in Moldavia without a woman visiting me, although many wanted to talk to me. I always refused to see them, saying I was ill. I experienced many temptations and sorrows from our foe, the devil, who still torments me."

"Well, dear Brother Sergius, one must spend many years in trials before reaching the state of John of Vorona. We must progress slowly, step by step. Those who want to reach the goal all at once are easily captured by the enemy and fall into spiritual delusion. Believe me, my friend, we need most and always humility. Without it disputations and dissensions are unavoidable. Everyone wants to maintain his own point of view and impose it on everyone else. In this way disputants part continually and imperceptibly farther and farther from the truth, incited by the devil. The startzy of Optino advised all to use the Prayer of Jesus vocally as a means to attain repentance while the Prayer of the Heart they advised to be used rarely and only by those who had overcome their passions and were under the guidance of an experienced staretz. The wise monks of Optino thought that it was too daring to practice the Prayer of the Heart before conquering passions. Such boldness can easily lead towards an incurable delusion. Be always humble, my friend, and you will never be ashamed."

A few days later, Father Ilian again visited me.

"I found in your library," I told him, "two manuscripts that interested me very much. The first is, most probably, the original of the well-known *Tales of a Russian Pilgrim,* and the second is *Notes of the Nun Panteleimona.*"

"Yes, our Russian manuscripts are still unsorted and I believe some good finds can still be made. We have no one to undertake the work of cataloguing them. The number of our monks decreases continually. There are not enough now even for the essential work."

"I have read *The Tales of a Russian Pilgrim* several times, Father Ilian. What do you think of them?"

"I think as Staretz Ambrose of Optino did when he wrote to a nun: 'There is nothing contrary to faith in *The Tales of a Russian Pilgrim.* The latter lived free, unbound by cares and duties. He practiced prayer in the way he wanted. For monks living in community and especially for those with responsibilities, his way of life is not possible. Cenobites, since they are bound by various duties, can practice the Prayer only when they are free; the rest will be completed by obedience.'"

"I believe, Father Ilian, that only hermits or pilgrims can really practice the unceasing Prayer of Jesus. Staretz Michael told me the same in Uusi Valamo. Here, on Athos, the unceasing Prayer of Jesus is practiced mostly by the hermits of Karoulia. Tell me, Father, why are nearly all your conventual offices performed at night?"

"Such is the ancient tradition. Saint Isaac the Syrian wrote: 'Every prayer that we say at night is more important than all our work during the day.' The sweet feeling so well known to one who fasts during daytime is a reflection of the light flowing from our nightly monastic labors. This is very important in order to pacify our continuous stream of thoughts, which can be vanquished only by repentance and unceasing prayer."

Once, I asked Father Ilian about the practice of the Prayer of Jesus in the world, whether it is good or not.

"It is good, my friend," Father Ilian answered. "Father John of Kronstadt was a parish priest and thanks to the Prayer of Jesus reached great saintliness and became a noted miracle worker and healer. He wrote in his book *My Life in Christ* that it is far better to say five words from the heart than to recite a multitude of prayers without attention and tender feeling. He also writes that when we pray, we must be full of attention in order that our inner man may pray with the outer. If not, the devil will occupy our attention during prayer with his distracting thoughts, especially blasphemous and impure ones. This happens to quite a few even in church and on festive occasions. We must not lose our courage and give up prayer but persevere in it. In due course the devil will retreat."

"Tell me, Father Ilian, can a busy man pray quickly and yet purely?"

"Yes, he can. The same Father John affirmed that those who had learned inner prayer might do so. For that, our heart must sincerely desire what we ask, feel the truth of the words pronounced and be simple and pure. Such a prayer does not suffer from hurry. But to those who have not attained the Prayer of the Heart, it is necessary to pray slowly, awaiting the response of the heart. Because, according to Father John, prayer is the elevation of mind and heart to God. It is clear that he who is attached to anything earthly, for instance to money, honors and the like or overcome by passions like hatred or envy cannot pray properly.

"And Father John also said very wisely: 'Remember always that the invisible is far more important in the world than the visible.' It is when something unseen leaves the living creature that it loses its life and turns into dust. We all live by the invisible energy of God. Whatever man loves, whatever he turns to, this he finds. If he loves earthly things and they settle down in him, he will become earthly himself and will be bound up by those same things. On the other hand, if he loves heavenly things they will dwell in his heart and will make him fully alive. When man has God always in his mind, it means that the Kingdom of Heaven has come unto him. Thus this man sees God everywhere and realizes his omnipresence, goodness, and mercy."

Another day when I was discussing with Father Ilian the writings of Father John of Kronstadt, he said to me: "Why are we so unhappy and anxious when we do not receive something desired or lose some treasure? It is because the wanted or lost thing was the idol of our heart and we have abandoned the Lord, the source of the living water that alone can quench our thirst. If we are really attached to God, neither our earthly losses nor an unfulfilled expectation in this life will sadden us. A fervent prayer accompanied with tears not only covers our sins but also heals our illnesses and weaknesses. The ascetic is truly renewed as an eagle. When we are young and strong and inexperienced, we are tempted to think that Christ is far away in heaven and the devil is far from us. But, with age, we find that Christ and the devil are nearby to help us or to harm us. When we pray mechanically, without attention and devotion, it means that our heart is full of unbelief and indifference. Our heart does not realize then our sinfulness and our pride. Anyone can find out whether he is proud or not. The more ardent prayer is, the humbler the man; the more mechanical, the prouder."

I left the monastery one warm day in May. Father Seraphim, the infirmarian, arranged a brotherly meal for me, inviting Father Ilian. We discussed for the last time various spiritual problems and monastic needs. Both of my brother monks wished to accompany me to the little port of the monastery, where I boarded the boat to Tripiti. When the boat started to move out to the open sea, I looked back to the harbor, where these two holy monks were standing on the sea wall.

I never saw Father Ilian again but I corresponded with him continually. He died on January 18, 1971. His secretary, Father Abel, wrote his obituary, published in the *Journal of the Moscow Patriarchate* in 1971. He was truly, as Father Abel wrote, "a son's loving Father." Always and everywhere he was an example to the community. He always used to come to the church first for all the conventual services and leave last. Even in the final days of his life, weighed down by illness, his strength visibly diminishing, he continued to attend all the services. The faults of his brothers he used to cover up with his love, punishing none. In this way he used to correct everyone.

Father Ilian died in his eighty-eighth year and was buried in his monastery with all the rites observed on the Holy Mountain.

CHAPTER 20

Father Nikon

In November, 1954, I traveled one day from the Russian Monastery of Saint Panteleimon to the Greek Monastery of Dionysiou. The day was warm and sunny as in late summer although it was already November. In the large motorboat there were only monks except myself and two workers. We navigated close to the coast with its monasteries and gardens. The first stop was at Daphni, the chief port of the Monastic Republic of the Holy Mountain. The motorboat from Tripite, the Greek port of embarkation for the Holy Mountain, stops at Daphni. Those who travel farther must change to another boat which goes on to the Skete of Saint Anne. We had about one-hour's wait for this second boat. I used this time to walk through Daphni. From Daphni a road leads up to Karyes, the capital of the Monastic Republic, and to several of the larger monasteries. On the embankment I saw two old monks sitting on a stone and talking to each other. One of the monks looked like Father Nikon, a former officer of the Russian Imperial Guard. After the Civil War in Russia he had retired to Mount Athos to live in a small monastery or *kellia* as they are called in Greek. I had met him many years previously in Oxford. He was already a monk and was traveling on the monastery's business. Mount Athos had suffered much since the collapse of the Empire and the advent of the Soviets and these small communities lived largely on the alms collected from the faithful around the world. I corresponded with him and met him occasionally afterwards. He realized that much traveling and continuous contact with the world are not good for a monk.

I approached the old monk and asked him: "Do you recognize me, Father Nikon?"

"Of course, I do, Sergei Nikolaevitch. But I do not live any longer in the *kellia* nor travel about as I did formerly. I live now as a hermit in Karoulia (an area at the tip of the Athonite Peninsula). I have been invited with my fellow hermit, Father Alexander, who is with me, to attend the monastic feast at Saint Grigoriou."

Saint Grigoriou is one of the large monasteries down the coast from Daphni. Father Alexander was a simple, peasant monk. He had been in Russia at the beginning of the First World War and had been prevented from returning to his beloved Holy Mountain for many years. He was now very happy to be back in the Monastic Republic.

I told Father Nikon that I had met two Athonite monks in the West. "Yes," he answered, "but that is not good." Father felt that a monk should not leave his monastery unless he is sent out by his superiors on lawful business and then only for a limited time. "It is not good for a monk to mix in politics," he said, "especially if that prevents him from returning to his monastery. Neither is it good to leave the Holy Mountain, changing from one monastery to another in search of an easier life. Many monks leave the Mountain for this reason. They destroy the Monastic Republic."

Father Nikon had been an officer and knew well from experience that once an officer begins to criticize the higher authorities and their commands discipline is lost. "Once an officer begins to be critical and unruly, the soldiers will be too. This was the situation on the eve of the Revolution in Russia. A monk is a soldier of Christ, who must obey his superiors and live a frugal, humble and self-effacing life. Comfortable, easy living was never good for monks. All history demonstrates this and it is as true in the East as in the West. Once monks begin to be well off, they degenerate. Many Latin monasteries provide a very comfortable life and that is dangerous. Many Russian monasteries in the Empire also lived far too well. And it should be noticed the richer the monastery is, the fewer vocations it attracts and they are not especially good ones.

"It is true, of course, that external observances alone cannot save us but slackness is equally bad," Father Nikon explained. "Penance, prayer, humility and charity are necessary for salvation but how can a well-fed, comfortably living man pray with the proper humility and a spirit of penance? Services and even private prayer will be monotonous for such a monk and cause boredom. He would prefer bold intellectual speculations in theology or long services to exercise his love and knowledge of music or any distracting activity that will keep him occupied."

Father Nikon felt that to pray well, to meditate fruitfully, one must live in Karoulia as a hermit in that dire poverty which generates humility and compassion. "The wealthy man rarely has compassion otherwise he would not be wealthy. He is usually indifferent to the suffering of others. It is for this reason that Christ said that it is difficult for a rich man to enter the Kingdom of Heaven.

"Isn't that true, Father Alexander?" Father Nikon asked his silent companion.

"Yes, it is true. The poor and oppressed have far more compassion and love than those who are well off," Father Alexander answered. "I noticed this during my troubled years in the Soviet Union. The newly rich Communist officials were hard on people."

I told Father Nikon what had happened to me in the intervening years. Father Nikon looked at me thoughtfully: "Well, my dear friend, everything in this world is vanity and vanity of vanities. None can find happiness, real happiness, in this world. Our parents, our dear ones, our friends, die. Our wealth is taken from us by others in wars and revolutions or we ourselves lose it. Anyone who wants to make a career in the world cannot avoid sins and intrigues. Even if he reaches his highest ambitions he finds out that it is more difficult to remain on the top than to reach it. Many other people want to reach the top and will not be particular about the means they use to throw down the one at the top. Therefore all worldly things lead to vanity and trouble of spirit. The wise Solomon wrote thus and he was right. True happiness is in wisdom, in the entire surrender of oneself to the Divine will."

"But how can we find the will of God for us?" I asked.

"Find in the library of Roussiko (Saint Panteleimon's Monastery) the small book of Saint John of Tobolsk, *Ilivtropion*. It was published in Kiev in 1890. They should have it. You will find there much useful and profitable advice.

"In order to carry out the will of God we must live according to that will as it is set forth in the Holy Scriptures, by the Church and by the circumstances of life. The pursuit of our own will is the root of all our sins and faults, when we surrender ourselves to our compulsions and passions knowing full well that they are displeasing to God. We always try to justify our passions pointing out that they are reasonable and useful. We justify our meanness, presenting it as wise economy. Our anger we interpret as a lawful defense of our personality or as a need to discipline our subordinates. We try to justify even the most brutal and animal compulsions. Saint John says: 'Everyone, who surrenders himself entirely to the will of God is truly free on every side. He is not depressed if he is unable to acquire something, nor if he loses something. He accepts the Divine will and submits himself to it.'"

"But how can we know what God wants from us?"

"When God allows something to happen which is very hard for us to accept, we must at once, and for good, sacrifice our own will and say: 'Thy will be done.' From that submission comes a wonderful courage and a tranquillity of soul hard to describe. He who truly hopes in God, fulfills all his duties, even the most painful without any anxiety. And he is never depressed. Depression is the result of weak faith. Everything is possible to him who believes. Of course," Father Nikon continued, "prayer is of paramount importance, as well as spiritual direction. No one is a good judge in his own case. We must ask the advice of wise and God-fearing men, especially the startzy."

"But can we find a staretz in our age, Father Nikon?"

"We can if we really look. You have met such monks in Finland and you may meet some here on Athos. In any case, we must ourselves pray with diligence. An old monk once said: 'Remain in your cell. It will instruct you in everything.' Look now, our motorboat is coming."

The motorboat stopped at the pier and we boarded it. The passengers were few, only monks. We left this haven. The sea was quiet and deep blue. The sunshine was strong and the air warm. Grigoriou was our first stop and nearly all the passengers left. Only six remained.

"We shouldn't attach ourselves to anything," Father Nikon said as we separated, "neither to our relatives nor to titles, power and wealth nor to scholarship. We have not here any abiding city. We should look for the world to come. God be with you!"

I never saw Father Nikon again.

CHAPTER 21

Father Euthemios

One day during my stay at St. Panteleimon's in 1954 Father Ilian suggested that I visit the Greek monastery of Dionysiou. He said they had a very fine library and, more important, there were some truly spiritual monks in the community. He especially urged me to speak with the hegumen, Archimandrite Gabriel, and the librarian, Father Euthemios. The latter, according to Father Ilian, was what is called a Fool for Christ or *yurodivini*. So one fine, sunny morning, I left St. Panteleimon's for Dionysiou.

The little boat took me first to Daphni, the port of Mount Athos and then on south. I looked back on the imposing mass of buildings that constituted St. Panteleimon's; all was bathed in warm October sunshine. After we passed Grigoriou, which is a picturesque monastery built on the very edge of the water, the coast became more and more rugged. The steep slope of the great mountain reached right down to the water's edge and the terrain became ever more wild. Here and there one could see small hermitages set into the mountainside.

"Look up," one of the monks said to me in Greek, "Simonos Petras!" I looked up. A white monastery with blue galleries, built boldly on a great rock, stood silhouetted against the dark blue sky. It was a hymn to God in stone. It looked to me like a Tibetan monastery. Simonos Petras certainly is not only picturesque but impressive. The boat rounded a promontory and the monastery quickly disappeared from sight. Soon we were approaching another, a grey-white citadel set high above its port on a rocky prominence. This was Dionysiou.

At the port, I disembarked, as did two Greek police officers. We started to climb up to the monastery along a steep, rough road. The officers began speaking to me. They said that their headquarters on Athos is in Karyes, the capital of the Monastic Republic, but they also have permanent police posts at three other monasteries: St. Panteleimon's, the Great Lavra and Vatopedi. The other monasteries they visit only from time to time. Their job is to control the movement of foreigners and to watch for smugglers of rare books and icons, many of which have been illegally removed from Athos to Greece. No book, manuscript, icon or any ancient ecclesiastical object may be taken from Mount Athos without proper permission.

We approached the gate of the monastery. It was already beginning to grow dark, but the gates were still open. A young monk met us and led us to the guest house. We crossed the inner court and went up a narrow staircase to the dining room where supper awaited us. The guestmaster, a Greek from Macedonia, spoke Bulgarian. Supper was lively because the monks treated police officers well. During our meal, a tall, ascetic-looking monk entered the room and, after saluting the company, addressed us in excellent Russian. He was Father Euthemios.

Born in Asia Minor, Father Euthemios went early to the Caucasus where he became a licensed accountant. He never married and after the Bolsheviks rose to power he left Russia and entered this monastery on Mount Athos. He could not return to his native Trebizond for all the Greeks had been expelled from there by the Turks after the disastrous Greco-Turkish War of 1922. Dionysiou was founded by Greeks from Trebizond many centuries before and natives of that city usually entered Dionysiou when they became monks on Mount Athos. Of the twenty sovereign monasteries on the Holy Mountain seventeen are Greek and each usually receives the natives from one well-defined region: Macedonia, Cyprus, Asia Minor, the Islands and so on. At the time of my visit, Father Euthemios was a librarian. He was not a priest. Priests are few in number in Athonite monasteries. As in earlier times, nearly all the monks are laymen.

"Do not stay here and talk for a long time," Father Euthemios said, "otherwise you will be late for the morning service in the church."

After Father Euthemios had left, the officers looked at each other and asked the guestmaster, "Who is that impressive monk?" "Our librarian," he answered. "He is a bit unusual, an eccentric or, as the saying has it, a Fool for Christ's sake."

It was late when I reached my room, a very large one, simply furnished. I stepped out on the balcony which overlooked the sea far below. The night was still and warm, the air pure and richly scented. "What peace and beauty!" I thought as I returned to my room and retired.

Father Euthemios was right! I overslept and missed the morning service. After dressing in the candlelight, I went down to the church. Passing along several dark corridors and staircases, I entered. Orthros had just ended. Some old monks dozed in the dark narthex, waiting to go back into the church for the Liturgy. The tall, dark figure of Father Euthemios appeared from nowhere.

"I told you yesterday," he said to me quietly, "to go to bed early so you would not oversleep, as you have done, but never mind; come with me." He then led me into the church. Only a few oil lamps flickered in the darkness. Father conducted me to the stall next to that of Father Superior and again disappeared into the darkness. The church had its own air of mystery. A few red lamps burned before the golden iconostasis and the icons on the stand. Hieratic saints solemnly looked down from the blue walls. It seemed as though they, too, had come to assist at the Liturgy, representing the church triumphant. Silence reigned except for the voice of the monk reading the prayers of preparation. An old priest came to ask my name in order to be able to mention it in the *proskomidia*. "Sergius is a good name," he said as he withdrew.

A very impressive monk, with the face of an ascetic and meditative eyes, entered the Superior's stall. It was Father Gabriel, hegumen of Dionysiou, one of the most revered figures in the Monastic Republic. The Liturgy began. It lasted several hours. The Byzantine chant was perfect in this old Athonite church. All notion of time and space vanished. It seemed as if time were no more, that we were in eternity with those saints on the walls, participating in the never-ending praise of God.

After Liturgy, Father Euthemios brought me to the hegumen's reception room and the usual refreshments were served. I told Father Gabriel about my latest journeys and my forthcoming visit to Patriarch Athenagoras in Constantinople. I also shared with him my impressions of Mount Athos and especially of Saint Panteleimon's. The hegumen told me it takes a few months at least and a stay in several monasteries to understand life on the Holy Mountain. He was glad that I had taken the first step.

"Prayer," he said, "is the most important thing; all other things are secondary even though they be necessary or even unavoidable." He wished me a happy and profitable stay on Athos as I took my leave.

I had several talks with Father Euthemios during my stay in Dionysiou. I soon realized that he was indeed a Fool for Christ's sake. He was very severe on himself and toward others. The slightest weakness brought a severe reproof. As I had already met some Fools for Christ's sake, I understood Father Euthemios' way of speaking. "The thing we need most," he said, "is humility and this cannot be acquired without much suffering. We love to be honored and made much of and we hate to be humiliated. It is painful to teach people humility, especially those in high positions. And yet they have most need of such lessons. If men do not teach them, God will by destroying them as happened with Hitler, Mussolini and many others. Even in the Church, even among bishops and abbots, there is far too much pomposity and intolerance. In Russia it disappeared because the Bolsheviks taught such a lesson that it will take a long time for anyone to forget it. The Communists are the scourge of God, sent to teach us the path of virtue."

Father Euthemios went on to recount a story. "There was once a holy monk known for his prophecies and there was a bishop who wanted to be Primate. One day the bishop called on the holy monk. The latter, seeing him, took no notice of him but continued his exercises, leaving the bishop standing at the door of his cell. The bishop, a proud man, became furious. 'Is this the way you treat bishops, proud monk?' he asked. 'It is not good for a bishop, my lord,' the monk answered, 'to take a monk from his prayer in order to engage him in vain and foolish conversation. Be humble and keep still. If you do so, you might well receive the Primacy but if you continue to act as you are now doing, trying to please people in high station, you will never attain the Primacy. Instead you will lose your diocese and be sent to do penance in a strict monastery under a harsh abbot. Do you understand what I am saying? Now you may go.'

"The bishop went to the abbot and complained: 'That monk is an uncouth and bold man. He offended me greatly. He should be punished.' 'Well, my lord,' the abbot answered, 'I told you that he is a Fool for Christ's sake, and says candidly what others hide in order to please people. I warned you not to consult him unless you wanted to be humiliated.'

"What the monk predicted actually happened. Instead of becoming Primate, the bishop was deprived of his diocese and sent to do penance in a monastery. After some years the bishop was freed and returned to consult the monk, this time very humbly. 'Well, my lord,' the monk remarked, 'you know now that pride and the favor of the great of this world lead to destruction. But as you have humbled yourself, you will be exalted though not in the way you think. Retire to a monastery and there you will experience spiritual joys of the highest order before which all earthly honors are nothing.'"

Father Euthemios assured me that he was rude to the hegumen

and others in order to keep them on the right road and that he had spoken severely to me on my arrival for the same reason. He went on to say: "Remember always, my friend, that humiliation is good for us and praise is bad. I wouldn't advise you to be rude to others, as I so often am, because you have another vocation but never try to please people by flattery. This is bad for them and for you."

I then questioned Father on my own behavior. Should one tell only the truth, neither minimizing it nor exaggerating? Such a course would not be easy, of course, but it seems to be the only way. Father agreed, and went on: "All lie, some more, some less, some openly, some discreetly. Because we commit sins all the time, we must pray all the time. This is the reason for the Jesus Prayer. Remember also that the harder life is for you, the better. Nowadays everybody looks for comfort and easy living but this is destructive to the soul and also to the body."

Such was the substance of my first long talk with this Fool for Christ.

"Avoid all daydreaming and vain speculation," Father Euthemios told me when for a second time we sat down for a discussion. "They do no good. The devil uses them to lead us into sin, suggesting that we do this and that, tempting us either to look for popularity and honors or to engage in worldly pursuits, money, comfort, and the like. The heart that is perfectly free from all such dreams is filled with divine and mysterious thoughts; they play in it, like fishes or dolphins in the deep sea."

This wise Fool went on to counsel, "A person should not try to speculate on theological subjects before his heart is purified. Otherwise he may very well fall into error or become an apostate. The Fathers have truly said, 'Every saint is a theologian and every theologian must be a saint.' It is quite easy to speculate and produce elaborate and seemingly correct systems of thought; living a holy life is a much more difficult task. In Greece, many theologians are educated in Athens and in Thessaloniki. These men like to speculate, but only a very few of them are ordained; they are not able to face the trials and difficulties of the priestly life or live up to the demands of the priestly state. They prefer to be schoolteachers. That promises to be an easier life."

At this point in our conversation, I asked: "Father, how do we fight against the tempting thoughts that come to us?"

"That is a wise question," he replied. "The continuous use of the Prayer of Jesus and watchfulness are the answer. We must keep our heart pure and avoid judging others. We must not be afraid of tempting thoughts. They will disappear in due course if we persevere in prayer and watching. Experience teaches us that. A true monk is one who has none but God in his heart. The monk who has something besides God in his heart is no longer a monk but an idolater, serving all kinds of devils: vanity, pride, mammon and so on. The inner man suffers much from external impressions and sensations. Nevertheless, prayer, humility and watchfulness over our thoughts will in due time repel all untoward thoughts and in the purified heart the Divine Light will begin to shine. And remember," Father added, "no one can approach God unless he leaves this world."

He went on to explain what he meant by this world, that whole complex of temptations and passions that beset one in ordinary human life. For a sensitive man, it is difficult to live in the world and to see constantly before him all kinds of sin and vice. The devil does his best to seduce people and draw them away from God, involving them in all kinds of preoccupations that leave no time to pray properly and meditate quietly. In the end, such unfortunate people come to the conclusion that prayer is of little value. Every good deed is for them a prayer, they maintain; one venerates God in serving one's neighbor. As a result, they begin to reduce their personal prayers and to neglect the services in the church. Little by little they begin to have a distaste for prayer and go to the services merely by custom or necessity. In the end they become virtual apostates. The easiest way to give up our faith is to cease to pray. And those who cease to pray become, in truth, unbelievers, although they may occasionally drop into church.

"If such be the case," I concluded, "there are very few Christians in the world, because only a few pray to God regularly and receive the sacraments well prepared."

Father Euthemios agreed. Real Christians have always been rare and nowadays still more so. But it is not our business to judge others. We must judge ourselves because each one must answer for his own deeds and not for those of his neighbor.

One evening we were sitting on the balcony of Father Euthemios' cell overlooking the sea. It was a mild autumn evening. We could see the sun slowly setting in the West. The sky and the sea were both a beautiful gold.

"Father Euthemios," I told him, "in Konevitsa I questioned Father Dorofey and Father Michael of New Valamo on the limit of prayer. And you, what do you say about this?"

"Even if the collective prayers in church or the ones said in the cell, read or chanted from books, are very useful, they are, by their very nature, intermittent. We do not always have books in our possession. We cannot spend all our time in church or in our cell. We must live and accomplish our duties. I do not know any prayer other than the Jesus Prayer that can be unceasing. For this prayer we do not have to be in church or in our cell or to have books. We can pray with it everywhere, in the house, in the street, on a trip, in prison, in a hospital and so on. We only need to learn it."

"But how do we learn this Prayer?"

"How is not important. At first repeat it by yourself in a low voice according to your own ability. Do this in your room, while going from place to place and when there is no one near you. One needs to repeat this Prayer slowly with attention in a low tone, as beggars solicit alms: 'Lord Jesus Christ, Son of God, have mercy upon me, a sinner.' Repeat this same prayer mentally but always slowly and attentively. Afterwards you can time it with your respiration and the beat of your heart. However, you should not do this without help. You must first find someone who practices this hesychastic prayer and he will show you what needs to be done. Otherwise you can fall into vain thoughts and illusions. Some years are needed to learn the prayer well. But with the grace of God one can rapidly master it. With time this prayer becomes perpetual. We can compare it with a stream which keeps flowing continuously while we walk, work or sleep. I sleep, but my heart is awake. Later on, you will no longer need words, nor thoughts. Your entire life will be prayer, as Father Dorofey said of Staretz John of Moldavia."

"Are there still men like Staretz John?"

"There are still some, undoubtedly. Even here on Mount Athos, at Karoulia, there are some hermits with much experience of this Prayer."

"Tell me, Father Euthemios, is it possible to recognize someone who has reached a high degree in the Prayer of Jesus?"

"Why not? Yes, it is possible."

"But how?"

"Well, if you desire to learn this Prayer, choose a humble and serene staretz, one who judges no one though he may be in some ways a Fool for Christ, one who never becomes irritated and who does not give orders to everybody. There are unfortunately some startzy who, having failed to master themselves, would like to direct others. They know the exterior aspect, the technique, as we might say, of the Prayer but not the spiritual aspect. Think about it for yourself: how can one who repeats continually: 'Have mercy upon me, a sinner' judge others?"

"Tell me, Father, which way of life is the highest?"

"To be a Fool for Jesus Christ of course. The wisdom of this world is foolishness before the Lord and vice-versa. But this style of life is the most difficult and one must not desire it without the counsel of a staretz."

"And what comes next?"

"The life as a pilgrim, similar to that of the author of *The Way of a Pilgrim*. For the world this is also foolishness. And afterwards the life of a hermit, a recluse, and a cenobite. But we must remember that the inner life is always superior to the exterior. There also exist some false Fools for Jesus Christ. There are some lazy pilgrims, some hermits full of illusions and some decadent cenobites. A person can be saved anywhere, even in the world. But it is easier in a monastery or in a hermitage where there is less temptation. But even in a monastery, if you do not pray properly, you will fall into a thousand vanities and puerilities. You will not only lose your spiritual treasures but you will become worse than you were in the world. One can even become an apostate. It happens."

"Will they soon ring the bell for vespers, Father?"

"Yes, soon," he replied. "There is the sound of the semantron. We must go to church." We left the balcony and went through the corridors and down the stairs to the Katholikon, which was flooded with the rays of the setting sun. The service was already starting slowly with the habitual modesty of Mount Athos. The choir was chanting:

> O Gentle Light of the holy glory of the immortal, heavenly, holy blessed Father, O Jesus Christ! Having come to the setting of the sun, having beheld the evening light, we praise the Father, Son and Holy Spirit: God. Meet it is for you at all times to be hymned with reverent voices, O Son of God, Giver of life. Wherefore, the world does glorify you.

During the night I went out onto the balcony of my cell and I looked at the sky with its numberless stars. Father Euthemios came towards me slowly. "You look towards heaven. Admire the splendor and the beauty of creation. Do not think too much about the means. A time will come when you will understand many things, when you arrive at the summit of prayer. It is impossible to understand everything with our discursive reason. We need illumination. In the world with all its cares and worries men and women do not see this beauty and celestial grandeur. May God pardon my comparison but they are like swine searching for acorns. They look only towards the earth and towards perishable things. True happiness and supreme beauty are open only to those who live in God. Yes, the power of prayer is full of grace. In comparison all the rest is dust, and vanity of vanities."

My last discussion with Father Euthemios took place on the eve of my departure. We were sitting on the balcony of his cell which overlooks the sea and as we talked the sun turned to gold and then sank beneath the horizon.

"Tell me, Father," I asked, "how difficult is it to attain to pure prayer?"

"Yes," he said as he gravely nodded his head, "it is very difficult indeed to acquire pure prayer. It takes many years. Without much effort and many sorrows, pure prayer cannot be established in the heart. No prayer can be won by easy and comfortable living. True prayer is possible only to him who has purified his heart with tears and sorrows. He who is pure of heart sees God. The Light of Tabor shines within him. He sees then what Motovilov saw when he discussed this very thing with Saint Seraphim of Sarov."

"Is it exceptional to see such things, Father?" I asked.

He replied: "It is exceptional surely in the sense that there are only a few people who have such purity of heart as to see the true Light. We do not take much care to obtain purity of heart because we prefer worldly things: power, wealth, popularity and the like. But if we reflect a bit we will see that all those things are uncertain and passing. They merely involve us in all kinds of vain activities and finally destroy us before the appointed time."

"What is impure prayer?" I asked.

Father answered very gently: "When alien thoughts and anxieties remain with us during our prayer, then our prayer is impure. We cannot attain pure prayer until we leave the world and its temptations behind. Only then our mind can dwell on holy things. While in the world, we cannot attain to pure prayer but we can be gradually purified by sorrows. If we endure sorrows manfully and humbly, they might well lead us to the gift of tears which will speedily wash away our imperfections. It is quite possible to be saved in the world, even for the rich and powerful but it is very difficult, as Christ said when speaking about the rich.

"If you want to be saved, realize your own frailty and weakness. Then you will realize that God helps us all the time and this will make your faith in Providence unshakable. He who believes in Divine Providence is always cheerful because God carries him in his arms."

I plied the saintly monk with one more question: "Do you think, Father, that short prayers are better than lengthy ones?"

"Yes, I think so," he answered. "The publican, the whore and the good thief obtained their forgiveness with a single short prayer. Use a short prayer but repeat it often with compunction and feeling. That is enough. But we must pray till we obtain the gift of tears. Then we can expect nothing more because God gives the gift of contemplation only to those to whom he wishes. It is enough if we obtain certainty of heart that our sins are forgiven. This feeling, combined with a perfect faith in Divine Providence, will make our lives a paradise here on earth. It is impossible to describe all this. It must be learned by personal experience."

"And can I hope to have such an experience, Father?"

"Why not? All things are possible to him who believes."

I left Dionysiou the next morning. It was sunny and warm. Sea and sky were a deep, deep blue. Father Euthemios accompanied me to the little port. The boat came in and I boarded it. Soon it began to move away from the shore. As I looked back, the tall figure of Father Euthemios stood still on the pier, his stern yet radiant face a benediction.

The boat moved along the Athonite coast. The lofty white walls of Simonos Petras appeared against the deep blue sky, all bathed in sunlight, something of a vision. We passed Grigoriou, then Daphni. In due course I arrived at Saint Panteleimon's. I told Father Ilian of my talks with Father Euthemios. Father Ilian listened attentively and then said simply: "He is a good monk." I never saw Father Euthemios again. He died the next year, 1955. But I think I would agree with Archimandrite Ilian. The most suitable epitaph for this Fool for Christ's sake would be: A Good Monk.

CHAPTER 22

Father Misael

I met Father Misael on Mount Athos in 1957 when he was the guestmaster of Saint Panteleimon. He was tall and straight, an intelligent man with a good memory, friendly and wise. He had arrived on Mount Athos in 1896. He liked to relate the story of his journey via Moscow on his way to the Holy Mountain at the time of the preparations for the crowning of the Emperor Nicholas II, whom he venerated as a saint.

I had a beautiful guest room in the monastery. There were paintings on the walls of the Emperor Alexander III with his wife Mary and of Metropolitan Filaret of Moscow. The doors leading to the balcony, which was covered by wisteria in bloom, were open. I could see below the vast buildings of this enormous monastery with its churches and the gardens. Beyond I could see the mountains and the azure sky, all lit by the morning sun. Sitting by a window, I was examining the manuscript of *The Tales of a Russian Pilgrim* which I had found in the archives of the magnificent library of the monastery. The manuscript was beautifully written by an experienced hand and the date of its entry in the archives was well before the date of the publication of *The Tales* by the Archimandrite of the Monastery of Kazan. I was intrigued to discover, in comparing the manuscript with the published text, that several passages were missing in the published text as well as two long tales.

There was a knock at the door and Father Misael entered the room. "I have asked Basil, our domestic, to bring you some tea and some bread and jam to comfort you a bit."

"You treat me too well, Father Misael. I even feel confused."

"My dear brother, how could I not treat you well? You are a rare visitor. Russian and Orthodox visitors are no longer as numerous as in former times. Only a few come nowadays and then only for short visits. We are visited by strangers from many countries, by Catholics and Protestants, but most often by people who are simply curious and without any religion. They come and they travel from one monastery to another. We must show them everything and we need someone here especially to do that.

"I see that you are busy with a manuscript. It is well written and in Russian."

"Do you know, Father Misael, that I believe this to be the original manuscript of *The Sincere Tales of a Pilgrim*. I think that the Pilgrim visited the Holy Mountain and wrote his tales for Father Jerome Solomentsev who was then Confessor here. When the Archimandrite of Kazan published this manuscript he made many omissions, even two long tales."

"Goodness! And why did he omit all of that?"

"The little omissions are easy to explain. The Pilgrim speaks harshly against professional theologians of whom some have become bishops. Such a critical mind was bound to displease the prelates and the Archimandrite of Kazan undoubtedly did not wish to have difficulties with the hierarchy. The Pilgrim strongly criticized the scholastic decadence that was being taught at the time. The two long tales were omitted so as not to upset the readers, especially the monks. After all, the manuscript was written by a layman and solely meant for his confessor, not for publication."

"What is being discussed in the omitted tales?"

"In the first one — which, by the way, we find at the beginning of the book — the Pilgrim tells how he spent the night at an inn of questionable character and how he was awakened when a *troika* being driven by a drunk coachman, collided with the house just beneath the window of the room where he slept. But in the manuscript, it tells how the Pilgrim was tempted by the woman of that inn and when sexual desire was awakened in him the usual unceasing Prayer stopped abruptly. The Pilgrim was saved from sin by the accident which is reported. The woman was paralyzed at the time of the accident but was later healed by the Prayer of the Pilgrim. The second tale concerns a young girl who was saved from a similar grave danger by the Jesus Prayer."

"Yes, the Jesus Prayer is a great thing, Sergei Nikolaevitch," observed Father Misael. "It really saves from death and from shame. And it is also true that the usual Prayer stops when voluptuous pleasure takes hold of you. It takes a great effort to continue it then."

"Well, then, how can people practice this Prayer?"

"A blessed marriage is one thing but the animal sexual desire aroused in the Pilgrim by this woman is another. It means a disordered life and also adultery. Naturally, the archimandrite thought that these tales might shock those who do not understand these things correctly. And you know what the person who scandalizes one of these little ones receives in punishment. It is taught in the Scriptures that it would be better for the seducer if he had not been born. The demon is very cunning. If he does not succeed with one snare, he invents another one. He can even make us perish by this great Prayer if we lack humility. Do you understand this?

"I knew Father Hilarion, the author of the book, *In the Caucasian Mountains*. Father Hilarion lived as a hermit in the Caucasus. His book has been published twice and it was well accepted by the ecclesiastical censors. But Father Hilarion was not a theologian by profession. Some of his texts were not as clear as they could have been and were open to wrong interpretation. However, his faith was wholly orthodox. His book came into the hands of two noble and well-educated monks, Father Anthony Bulatovitch of the Skete of Saint Andrew and Father Alexis Kyreevsky of our monastery. And they started to dispute between themselves. According to Father

Anthony the book of Father Hilarion was the summit of wisdom but according to Father Alexis it was full of heresies. Many monks were gradually involved in their dispute and it led to a major disorder. In the end some hundreds of Russian monks were deported from Mount Athos to make it possible to reestablish good order. This was followed by the outbreak of the First World War and the Revolution. The number of Russian monks on Mount Athos started to decline until today there are only a few elderly monks here. There are no young men in our monastery. If Father Anthony and Father Alexis had been truly concerned with the Jesus Prayer in full humility of heart, they would never have started to dispute. The absence of humility renders the prayer superficial and external. It then becomes a pretense for real prayer. Dissension in a religious community means the absence of brotherly charity which depends on true, humble and continuous prayer. He who is proud, intolerant and authoritarian should not practice the Jesus Prayer if, while praying, he continues to sin all the time and does not repent. In such a case this Prayer leads to condemnation just as when one approaches the Sacrament of the Eucharist unworthily."

"How, Father Misael, can we recognize one who practices the Jesus Prayer correctly?"

"It is very easy to recognize such a man. He judges no one. I was told the following about Father Isaaky, Archimandrite of Optino:

> When the monks came to him to complain, one against the other, he would listen to them with attention. Then he would say,
>
> "What! He said that! And furthermore he hit you. This is very wrong and intolerable in a monastery."
>
> And then he would say, "Now go, Father, to the one who offended you and who hit you and beg him to forgive you."
>
> "But, he is the one who has offended me and who has hit me."

182

"Quite so! And Christ said: To him that beats you on the one cheek offer him the other. You are full of keenness to strike your brother. He could not offend you without some fault on your side. How far did you provoke your brother? Go and ask him to forgive you."

"Father Isaaky judged no one. If Father Anthony and Father Alexis had imitated him none of that sad story would have occurred. Always be at peace, brother Sergei, and you will be saved."

Part V

France

In 1955 Serge Bolshakoff made acquaintance with Father Tikhon Voinov. Father Tikhon also had to leave Russia in 1919 as an emigrant. In his old age he entered a small Orthodox monastery in Paris and became a monk. It was here that Doctor Bolshakoff met him.

CHAPTER 23

Father Tikhon Voinov

My friendship with Father Tikhon extended over a period of seven years. I used to discuss many problems of spirituality with him either in Paris or in Villemoisson. Father Tikhon was born in 1882. His father was an officer in a Don Cossack regiment. His mother was a Pole. He received a very good education at home and at school and became an officer in the Staman Guard in Saint Petersburg. He gave me very interesting accounts of life among the guards and at the Imperial Court at Saint Petersburg at the beginning of the century. He graduated from the Academy of the General Staff and became in 1914 the youngest colonel in the Imperial Army, being only thirty-one years old. He survived the First World War as well as the Civil War and in 1919 became an emigre. He was obliged to work for his living as a semiskilled laborer. As old age crept up on him, he was retired with a pension. He then entered a small Orthodox monastic community in Paris. During the time I was acquainted with Father, this community moved to Villemoisson, about eighteen miles from the French capital.

Father Tikhon had suffered much in his life but this did not embitter him; rather, it transformed him into a loving old monk much given to prayer and good works. There was something of Father Ilian in him but there were also many differences. Father Tikhon habitually practiced the Prayer of Jesus and entered very deeply into it even though he did not have an experienced guide.

I first met Father Tikhon in March, 1955, soon after my long journey to Konevitsa, Uusi Valamo and Mount Athos. In 1957 I visited Mount Athos once again. In 1960 I visited the Lavra of the Holy Trinity in Zagorsk and Pskovo-Petchersky Monastery in the Soviet Union. My acquaintance with Father Tikhon coincided then with the period when I was able to consult with Father Dorofey in Konevitsa, Father Luke and Father Michael in Uusi Valamo and Pskovo-Petchersky and Father Ilian on Mount Athos. I discussed with Father Tikhon my impressions, what I saw, heard and read. We used to converse almost exclusively on spiritual subjects. Father Tikhon usually avoided both small talk and reminiscences but when he did engage in them they were, I must say, most interesting and colorful.

It was Father Tikhon's opinion that we neglect the "signs," that we do not meditate sufficiently on our past, out of which comes our present and future. He thought, too, that we are neglectful in regard to meditating on our own names and the lives of the saints after whom we are named. Occasionally Father would write down his own meditations which I found to be both deep and to the point. For him, nothing happened in the world without Divine Providence. Nothing in the world was purposeless or insignificant. Each person, thing and event had their meanings. And all this was to be taken into consideration. In the world, Father Tikhon had been named Nicholas, which means "victor," and his name in religion, Tikhon, means "happiness." He used to say: "I was a soldier but failed to realize the meaning of my name, to vanquish my passions and sins, and I was defeated in my life. Becoming a monk and receiving a new name, I found happiness."

Meditating on the apparition of the Savior to Saint Mary Magdalene after his Resurrection, Father Tikhon underlined the fact that she recognized the Lord only when she turned back, looked fixedly at him and he called her by name: "Mary!" According to Father Tikhon, if we truly meditate on our past, we can easily see Divine Providence guiding our lives and realize that Christ is always with us, till the end of the world.

As an infant, Father Tikhon had been baptized into the Orthodox faith but he lost it early and became an unbeliever. However, the atheistic explanation of the world and life did not satisfy him so he searched first among the theosophists and the occultists and then among the extreme Protestant sects. In due course he returned to the faith of his childhood. Later, a widower and retired, he became a monk. Still, some of the theological ideas of Father Tikhon were as daring as those of Teilhard de Chardin and often scandalized simple monks. But Father Tikhon never overstepped the boundaries of Orthodoxy once he returned to faith.

Father Tikhon was a humble monk, simple in his ways and always ready to listen and to help others. Many people came to him for advice. He was not unlike a true staretz. I often shared with him extracts from the writings of Eastern Christian mystics. He fully accepted the view of Saint Isaac the Syrian that we cannot approach God in any other way than by unceasing prayer which was for Father Tikhon a great joy. Continuous visits by many people were for him a true cross because they prevented him from speaking to God in unceasing prayer. While people usually came to him for advice or consolation, some abused Father Tikhon's kindness with idle talk or even condemnation of other people. The latter talk he usually stopped at once and was unwilling to receive again those who spoke in this way.

Father Tikhon was happy when I shared with him quotations from Saint Seraphim of Sarov. He especially liked these passages:

> Perfect love for God unites lovers with God and among themselves.
>
> Minds that have acquired spiritual love must never dwell on anything contrary to this love.
>
> Solitude, prayer, love and abstinence are the four wheels of the vehicle that carries our spirit heavenward.

Subdue the flesh with fasts and vigils and you will be able to reject the cunning suggestions of concupiscence.

As it is God's business to rule over the world so it is the soul's business to rule over the body.

Concupiscence is destroyed by suffering and sorrow either voluntarily undertaken or received from Providence.

With what measure you master your body, with that same measure God will recompense you with the hoped-for good.

Father Tikhon usually interpreted these in this way: "We must rule over our body and never allow the latter to dominate us because, if we do, we become a toy of all the passions and vices. I witnessed all that in my own experience and in the lives of others."

Other passages Father Tikhon especially liked are the following:

If an ascetic desires the future as if it were already present, altogether forgetting everything earthly and more and more trying to experience the future life, this is a sign that he lives with true hope.

Impassibility is good. God himself grants and strengthens this state in the souls of those who love him.

Do not be lazy in the active life and your mind will be enlightened.

Solitude and prayer are the greatest means to acquire virtues; purifying the mind, they make it able to see the unseen.

"Well, Brother Sergius," he once said to me, "you told me that Father Michael used to answer your questions before you asked them. He already knew what you would ask. Only hermits and recluses receive such a gift. For them it is not guesswork as with us sinners. It is clairvoyance. Life in Christ demands of us a continuous vigilance over ourselves and this is attained only by unceasing prayer. I would like very much, my friend, to have a few talks with a staretz but they are very few now and I am old and an invalid."

One day I encouraged Father Tikhon to say something about silence. He responded: "Truly, my dear friend, silence is a great virtue. There is an icon called 'The Angel of Holy Silence.' For a monk, especially an old one, the cell is like the Babylonian furnace burning up the old man of flesh. In the cell, by silence and by watching over our thoughts, we approach God for it is said: 'Remain in your cell and it will teach you everything needful.' The cell makes an angel out of a man of flesh and blood. It introduces into us serenity of mind which is nothing more than a foretaste of the Kingdom of God. I now understand so well what Staretz John of Vorona says: 'I can hardly be with people now and especially with lay folk.'"

"Father Tikhon, with your love of prayer and solitude, is it hard for you to receive people who come to you for advice?"

"Yes, it is hard but necessary. We must bear each other's burdens. How can I expel these people? Especially here in Villemoisson which is not a desert. Many people live around us. Often talks are bad for me because the devil pushes me into daring philosophical speculations and then forces me to defend my questionable thesis and so scandalize others. This is a serious sin. The Fathers used to say that every saint is a theologian and every theologian must first be a saint. We overlook this truth and enter into disputations before we have mastered our passions. The result is divisions, schisms, heresies and apostasy. We should prove the truths of faith by our humility and good living and not with cunning human speculations."

"What would you say, Father Tikhon, of the following saying of St. Seraphim:

If a man does not worry too much about himself for the
love of God and for virtue, knowing that God takes care
of him, such a hope is true and wise. But if a man trusts

solely in his works and prays to God only when sudden and unforeseen misfortunes overtake him, for he sees no means to save himself, then his hope is vain and false. True hope seeks only the Kingdom of God and is sure that everything earthly that is necessary for this passing life will be indubitably granted. Our heart cannot be at rest until it has learned such a hope. The latter tranquilizes it completely."

"That is correct, dear Brother. You and I know this from personal experience and yet we fall frequently into vain thoughts, imagining that we can do something without God's assistance. In our contemporary world God, we may say, is completely forgotten. If anyone turns to God in prayer it is usually a sign that every human hope has been lost. Of course such a way of acting is vain and false. Generally speaking, we attain peace of mind only by passing through sorrows because the route to God is through them. I know perfectly well that I would not have come to God or become a monk if I had not experienced many hard trials which lasted for many years.

"I consider the infallible sign of a spiritual man to be his dwelling within himself, his interiority; that is, keeping guard over thoughts and unceasing prayer. When a man attains to peace of mind he can, like Father Michael, radiate serenity to others. Once we attain peace of mind we must keep it intact and never get excited when we are offended or humiliated. I am still unhappy when I am misunderstood or blamed. And although I hardly ever judge other people, I occasionally tolerate idle talk because I am still only a novice in true silence."

"What do you think of tears, Father Tikhon?"

"They are a great grace. There is nothing worse than stony indifference in prayer. Prayer without tears is cold, sad prayer. Tears melt away our insensibility and destroy our passions. Tears must not be despised. Among military people, brought up on stoicism, tears are considered to be shameful. Tears lead us to repentance and allow us to come through the most devilish temptations, preserving deep peace of soul in which the devil cannot sow his seeds. When we maintain peace of mind we can easily discover his insinuations. When our heart is in turmoil the devil has full freedom. Therefore we must never undertake anything when our soul is sorely vexed and anxious. We must wait till our heart becomes quiet again, and then act."

In the spring of 1962 I had a very strange dream, which I described to Father Tikhon. "I think," the monk observed, "that this dream will come true. Yet as a rule we must not trust in dreams, forebodings, et cetera, but ignore them. It is so easy to err and become superstitious. Still, if dreams lead us toward a good deed, they might be taken for guidance. In such a case they may come from above as we read in Scriptures and in the lives of the saints. Because I was in intimate relationship with occultists for a number of years, I saw and heard a great deal. It is inadvisable and often dangerous to probe into the future, especially by our own will.

"We must preserve our purity of heart: 'Blessed are the pure of heart for they shall see God.' Nor should we open our heart to many people but only to our Spiritual Father. In the latter case our treasure remains safe from foes, visible and invisible. This discretion is especially necessary if we have passed through great spiritual experiences. I read of this in the Fathers and also have learned it by my own experience."

"Father, have you read the instruction of Saint Seraphim on how to distinguish between good and evil thoughts as they come to us? He says:

> When a man receives something divine he rejoices in his heart but when he accepts something devilish he is troubled. The Christian heart receiving something divine does not demand confirmation from outside that the gift comes from the Lord because the experience itself persuades the heart that the suggestion is from heaven. The

heart feels within itself the fruits of the Spirit: love, joy, peace, long-suffering, goodness, charity, faith, meekness and abstinence, as the Apostle Paul wrote to the Galatians. Whereas if the devil comes to us even in the form of an angel of light and suggests the apparently most innocent ideas, the heart nevertheless will experience some obscurity and confusion in its thoughts and turmoil in its feelings. Thus by the very different results produced in his heart a man may distinguish between the divine and the diabolical.

"Isn't this so, Father Tikhon?"

"This is perfectly true, my friend. When I associated with the occultists, I saw many astonishing things that seemed good and yet I felt within my heart something disturbing, some confusion."

"The late Sergei Paul, Father, who before his return to the Church consorted much with the Sufis, said the same thing. I met his theosophical friends occasionally and I must say that my impression was similar. I felt the same thing while reading Tibetan books. One feels that there is something hidden, unsaid, esoteric."

"It is well, Brother Sergius, that you were not attracted to those things, which have the power to captivate people. I believe it is far easier to convert to Christ a militant atheist who is often really ignorant and a superficial thinker than a theosophist who is often the prisoner of some invisible power. The Tibetans do not deny the existence of such powers. They attribute things to the influence of the shamans. As far as we are concerned we should not accept anyone but Christ. To play with spiritism of any kind is dangerous indeed. Anyone who denies that Christ is the Son of God and the only Savior is an Antichrist according to the Apostle. The Church teaches nothing different. We save ourselves by humility, unceasing prayer and by love of God and our neighbor. We perish when we fall into daring speculations as the Gnostics did and neglect to lead a holy life."

One of my conversations with Father Tikhon took place in the spring, on the Day of Ascension, during the month of May. It was a warm and sunny day. The lilac had almost finished flowering and we could already see some small apples and pears on the fruit trees. I was sitting with him on a bench in the garden.

"How good God is!" observed Father Tikhon. "How delightful! Why not live and rejoice? The one who practices the Jesus Prayer, like the Pilgrim of whom you know, always has spring in his soul. He is not attached to anything. We must live neither in the past nor in the future. We must live in the present. We must live today and thank God for everything. We must understand that everything passes. My heavenly patron, Saint Tikhon of Zadonsk, wrote:

> Everything in this world is like flowing water. I was a child and an orphan. That passed. I attended school as a poor boy, badly clothed, and I was scorned. That passed as well. I ended my studies at a great seminary as first of the class and I became a professor. People then started to respect me. That also passed. I was named Archimandrite of a great monastery and also superior of a great seminary. People then started to flatter me. That passed. I was consecrated Bishop and traveled in a six horse-drawn coach. I was received at the Imperial Court. I saw many things, good and bad. People flattered me more and more. That passed. I resigned. People then started to oppress me. Then illness came. That also passed. Now it is old age and then it will be eternal rest.

"There, Sergei Nikolaevitch, lies our life. I was born into a rich family. I studied in an aristocratic school. I became an officer in the Imperial Guard. I was received at Court. I knew Leo Tolstoy. I drank abundantly of the cup of life. All that passed. Then I had some painful experiences. Some difficulties at the Officers Staff School, marriage with a divorcee, some intrigues, the Military Tribunal. Griefs and sorrows. That passed as well. I was found to be innocent and was well compensated. I was named colonel and I was the youngest colonel in Russia. But I had lost all interest in a military career. I had come to understand that everything passes, everything breaks, everything becomes weary. Then came the First World War, the Revolution, the Civil War, the emigration, a very serious illness which nearly took my life, then the very painful and incurable illness of my wife, followed by her death. Then the hard toil of work in Paris. All of that passed. All these sufferings and sorrows led me to faith and to a monastic life. I learned the art of unceasing prayer and I am always cheerful. Without all those sorrows and hard ordeals I would not have come to faith."

"Tell me, Father Tikhon," I asked the monk, "how can we attain peace of soul and how can we avoid useless regrets and illusory ambitions?"

"In the way I have already told you. Live in the present, there is no need to add to the troubles each day brings. And attach yourself especially to the Prayer. A new and wonderful world will then be opened before you.

"How shall I put it? You know the moths seen at night; they appear grey and uninteresting to us but to other moths with eyes organized differently to ours they appear extraordinarily beautiful, brilliant and glittering in all the colors of the rainbow. It is the same for those who are illuminated like the Pilgrim. The world appears different to them than it does to us. They see in everything the majesty of the Creator and his infinite mercy. When the Prayer becomes unceasing an indescribable joy occurs and at the same time the comprehension of the essence of things. This is impossible to describe. We can understand this only through experience."

"Is it possible to fall into pride?"

"Yes, it is very easy. But it is also possible to avoid such a fall. Saint Macarius the Great teaches that it is possible to be saved while lacking many virtues but without humility salvation is impossible. The publican and the good thief lacked all the other virtues and were saved exclusively by their humility. Satan possessed all the best things pos-

196

sible but he did not have humility and he fell. Meditation is good, also reflection upon the great mysteries which surround us but we must also have humility and must not judge others. Otherwise, we expose ourselves to great dangers. The heretics were men with great natural gifts but they lacked humility. In their own wisdom they revolted against the Church and perished."

"I read, Father Tikhon, that the Tibetan hermits who practice the repetition of the mantra: *Om mani padme oum*, that is "Treasure of lotus, I salute you," arrive gradually at great serenity and even ecstasy. When they reach a certain point, they start to shorten the mantra. Finally, one night, they come out of their cavern and looking at the grandeur of the sky full of stars, they say, "O," and they contemplate, immobilized, the majesty of the sky full of stars. Albert Einstein, the great physicist, replied as follows when asked if he had faith: 'Yes, if this means astonishment before the wisdom and majesty which rule in the cosmos.' But he did not accept dogmas. What do you think about that, Father Tikhon?"

"It is not for us to judge the visions of the Tibetan hermits nor the way in which Einstein understands the divinity. We have the Holy Scriptures, the *Philokalia* and the experience of a multitude of ascetics. Let us practice the Jesus Prayer humbly with patience. And at the appropriate time we will understand what is permitted for us to know if we do not grow weak. The principal thing towards which we must direct our course is love, love of Truth, in other words God, and love of our neighbor. At the Last Judgment we will not be questioned on the manner of our prayers or contemplation but we will be asked if we have fed, dressed and visited our neighbor. It is for those reasons that we will be condemned or justified. God is love. It is by this that we distinguish ourselves from the Hindu and Buddhist ascetics. With them, the principal thing is knowledge and evil is ignorance; but for us, the principal thing is love.

"This does not mean that contemplation is not important. It is well adapted for the elderly who no longer have the strength for acts of mercy in the active life and also for those who have been selected

197

by God to stand before him. But even the hermits should not separate themselves completely from others but should give written or oral answers to spiritual problems when they are questioned. All of the great hermits did that: Anthony, Macarius and many others. Everything must be done with discretion."

Father Tikhon died in 1964. He was in search of God for many years and finally he found him. He never seemed to reach the depth of Father Michael or the radiant joy of Father Ilian but everyone has his own vocation. Perhaps this lack of depth was due to his theosophical connections. We hardly realize how much our past influences us and how difficult it is to discard the habits of thought followed for years. Still there is great merit in detaching oneself from a sinful past and returning to the house of God. This Father Tikhon did. And when he did, he strove with great humility to be wholly a man of God and a servant of man. And for this reason I have no doubt as to his great holiness and the wisdom of his teaching.

At Journey's End

We may be feeling a bit fatigued at this point. It has been a long journey from the frozen northern reaches of Russia and Finland to the balmy shores where the waters of the Aegean lap the outcroppings of the Holy Mountain. And for us from the West it may have been a rather disconcerting journey, too. No nice systematic order here. No clearly marked trail up the mountain or from mansion to mansion in the interior castle. Not even a good orderly synthesis at the end.

No! For any approach such as that would certainly betray the wondrous rich tradition which these pages have allowed us to tap into. We can indeed be grateful for the intimate experience of this centuries-old and very alive tradition that we have been given as we were privileged to travel along with this pilgrim of the twentieth century, the young and not-so-young Serge Bolshakoff. We probably will never forget the wise words of Father John, the warm hospitality of Father Ilian. And we may well hope we never encounter a Fool for Christ like Father Euthemios — such a man of God is a bit too frank for our comfort. We have been brought into an authentic experience of how the treasures of this tradition have been handed down through the centuries: seekers seeking the sacred depositories, the spiritual fathers and mothers, and in chance conversations or more serious and soul-searching interviews drawing out nuggets that may indeed include more than one pearl of great price.

Bolshakoff paid a price for these treasures he gathered together and sought so generously to share with us. His journeys were not easy ones. I know from my own days on the trails of the Holy Mountain some of the price paid by such a pilgrim. Bolshakoff embraced the exile forced upon him and never again in the course of his long life enjoyed the comfortable security of a place called home but ever remained the pilgrim in quest of true wisdom. And we, too, must be ready to pay a price if there would be treasures here for us. For when we first encounter a treasure that has lain hidden it usually comes forth from its hiding place with its beauty and true worth fairly well obscured. Its true value will reveal itself to us only when it has been scoured by diligent reflection and allowed to begin to be a living reality in our own lives.

These Fathers of the Orthodox East do not mince words. Although the very positive character of our pilgrim spoke only of sunny days and azure skies, the cost of true discipleship is not obscured. As Christians our way is the humble way of dragging the cross, the daily cross. Nonetheless, with care not to engender false hopes, the Fathers do not hesitate to point to the summit of Tabor. We are all called to be transformed by that deifying light.

May these pages, more so on a second and third and fourth reading, disclose to each one of us their treasure, the words of life that will guide, encourage and strengthen us for the journey to that summit where we shall come to perceive and know by experience what the Fathers could not and did not attempt to express but which is the inmost source of the luster of all they do put into the words that our dear ecumenical pilgrim has brought to us.

We owe a debt of gratitude to the four who have gathered up these fragments from the heritage of Doctor Bolshakoff. Their very diversity, amazing indeed, gives a powerful witness to how wide was the influence of Bolshakoff and the power of this tradition to speak to what is deepest in the human spirit no matter what be our geographical location, our ethical background, our faith commitments. Hans Smith, born in Sukabumi, Indonesia, in 1926, was a teacher in Holland for thirty-six years and still lives in The Hague. He is not a member of any religious denomination yet he was in frequent correspondence with Serge Bolshakoff from 1984 to 1990. Victor Gareau, a Roman Catholic, had an equally long correspondence with our pilgrim. Victor is Canadian, born in 1947, a civil officer of the Canadian government since 1970. Dr. Anthony Spalding, also a Roman Catholic, was a personal friend of Serge Bolshakoff for over thirty years. Born in London in 1928, Spalding was a general practitioner in the East End of London for twenty-five years. The fourth of the compilers, Miroslaw Ryzyk, was born in Poland in 1963. Since 1984 he has worked as a maintenance engineer for the Polish Telecommunication in Bialystok where he lives. Like Serge, Miroslaw is a member of the Orthodox Church. Three of these four are married men and have enjoyed home and family. All of their lives have been enriched by the teaching that Dr. Bolshakoff has brought to them to such an extent that they not only felt obliged but had a great desire to share this richness with others as a tribute to a great ecumenical pilgrim.

If we could all begin to live at the deeper level to which these writings invite us and be enlightened by that deifying light, could we not then have a sure hope that the new millennium will see the fulfillment of the Lord's prayer: "That they all may be one, Father, as you in me and I in you, that they may all be one in us"?

Fr. M. Basil Pennington, o.c.s.o.
Saint Joseph's Abbey
Spencer, MA

Glossary

Akathistos (or *Acathist*) - A hymn. A service of praise in honor of the Holy Mother of God or of a saint.

Analogion - A free-standing, slanted bookstand, usually covered with cloth, on which service books or icons are placed during the services or permanently.

Archimandrite - Highest rank of a monk-priest, before that of a bishop.

Cenobitic - The monastic life which involves living in common obedience to a superior.

Dobrotolyubie - Literally "Love of beauty." The Russian version of the *Philokalia*.

Doukhovnaya - Spiritual illusions.

Dyadka - Personal servant.

Edinovertsy - Those Orthodox who practice the old rites in force before the liturgical reforms of Patriarch Nikon in the seventeenth century. They are also known as Old Ritualists or Old Believers.

Epitrachelion - A long, narrow vestment looped around the neck and hanging down in front which the priest wears when fulfilling the functions of his priestly office. It is the equivalent to the stole of the Latin priest.

Hegumen - Head of an autonomous monastery, somewhat similar to an abbot in the West, although he need not be the spiritual father of a community. He is usually elected by the community.

Hesychasm - A quality of stillness or silence. This term can be interpreted at many levels: exteriorly, meaning solitude or withdrawal into a cell; interiorly, a certain return to oneself, inner silence, spiritual poverty, a listening to God. A term used to denote Eastern Orthodox mysticism, particularly the practice of mental prayer or prayer of the heart. It is derived from the word *hesychia*, which means quiet, stillness, because such prayer requires the greatest inner and outer quiet or stillness for its effective practice and the attainment of its ultimate goal, which is union with God.

Hesychast - One who practices or has entered into a life of hesychasm.

Hierodeacon - A monk who is a deacon.

Hieromonk - A monk who is a priest

Iconostasis - A partition, usually with three openings, set between the nave and the sanctuary in Eastern Christian Churches. It is covered with many icons arranged according to a set pattern.

Idiorrhythmic - A style of life, adopted in some of the monasteries, where the monks receive an allowance from the common income, retain their property and do not have a common superior.

203

Izba - A hut in the woods.

Jesus Prayer - A brief ejaculatory prayer drawn from Scripture addressed to Jesus usually taking this form: 'Lord Jesus Christ, Son of God, have mercy on me, a sinner.'

Katholicon - The principal church of a monastery.

Lampadas - An oil lamp burning in front of an icon.

Lavra (Laura) - Originally a monastery which followed the rule of Saint Anthony, later it was used simply to designate certain large monasteries. Beside Kiev, there were eight monasteries in Russia which bore this title and there is the Great Lavra on Athos.

Liturgy - While this term is used in the West to refer to the whole of the public worship of the Church, among the Orthodox and in this book it refers to the Eucharistic Sacrifice.

Mandorrhason - A wide-sleeved cloak.

Mandya - An ample cloak worn by professed monks and nuns during services.

Megaloschemos - A monk who has received the great or angelic habit. This is the highest form of monastic profession. Originally there was only one monastic profession and one monastic habit or schema but in time a variation of grades developed, hence the distinction between the little and the great schema. Commonly there are three degrees of monastic profession accepted in the East: *rassophore*, *microschemos* and *megaloschemos*.

Metanias - Prostrations and bows made in prayer.

Metropolia - The Russian Orthodox Church in America, which has been recognized by the Russian Patriarch as an autocephalous church, i.e., independent of the Patriarchate and having its own head, the Metropolitan.

Monastic Republic - The monasteries on the Greek peninsula dominated by Mount Athos form a semiautonomous State of the Holy Mountain. The federated monasteries elect a synod to rule the peninsula.

Orthros - One of the principal services prayed by the Orthodox, usually at dawn.

Ougomonitsya - Inner stillness.

Ouverenie - A divine sign.

Panikhida - A service of prayer for those who have died. A memorial service.

Phelonion - A large outer vestment worn by an Eastern priest when he is fulfilling his more important functions. It is roughly equivalent to the chasuble of Western Christian vestiture.

Philokalia - A collection of patristic and hesychast writings concerning inner prayer and the monastic life forming a masterly summary of Orthodox mystical and ascetical teaching. It was compiled by Saints Macarius of Corinth and Nicodemus the Hagiorite and first published in Venice in 1782. It was translated into Slavonic under the title *Dobrotolyubie* by Saint Paissy Velichkovsky. Later, it was translated into Russian by Theophan the Recluse.

Poustyna - A place of retirement, literally a desert.

Prayer Cord (*komboschinion* or *tchotki*) - A prayer cord used by monks and by lay people in their prayers, especially when they are praying the Jesus Prayer, not so much to keep count, although that is part of it, as to facilitate attention. It is usually made of black wool, although sometimes strands of other colors or colored beads are added for decoration. In a properly made cord each knot is very carefully and prayerfully made with much symbolism going into its construction. The usual cord has one hundred knots separated into sections of twenty-five by a bead and having as a pendant a woven cross. A full cord of three-hundred knots might be used in the cell and a smaller one of fifty in the pocket. There also exists a prayer cord of thirty-three knots for lay people.

Proskomedia (*Prothesis*) - A ceremony performed before the celebration of the Liturgy at a table on the left side of the sanctuary where the priest prepares the bread and wine that is to be used in the Liturgy. Part of the ceremony involves cutting small pieces of bread and placing them on the diskos or plate while asking the Lord to remember particular intentions. In this way the priest brings the particular intentions of the faithful to the Liturgy.

Pustin - A small isolated monastery often dependent on a larger monastery.

Rassophore - The lower level of a Russian monk after the novitiate. The monk is tonsured but takes no vows.

Schema - The monastic habit. There are two kinds signifying the two higher degrees of the monastic life: the little schema and the great or angelic schema which implies a stricter life of asceticism and prayer.

Schimonk (or Schimnik) - A monk who has received the great schema.

Sereyenka (Serezha, Serezhenka) - Familiar term for Serge. Sergius, Sergei, and Serge are all variations of the same name.

Simandron (or Semantron) - A board that a monk carries about the monastery striking it with a wooden pallet to announce the services.

Skete (Skite) - A small monastic village where the monks live alone or in small groups and have a common church where they celebrate the Liturgy together. There is no limit to the size of a skete and some on Athos have had over 600 members.

Sobesednik - Interlocutor.

Starchestvo - A practice whereby the monk reveals to his staretz all his inner thoughts, intentions and temptations and receives his counsel.

Staretz (plural Startzy) - Spiritual father or monk distinguished by his piety, long experience of spiritual life and gift for guiding souls.

Stavrophore - or *microschemos* is a lower degree of monastic profession, between that of the *rassophore* and the *megaloschemos*.

Tales of a Russian Pilgrim - An alternative title to the work better known as *The Way of a Pilgrim*.

Taramandyas - Similar to the Latin little scapular.

Umilenie - A warm heart brought about in the person practicing interior prayer by a touch of the Holy Spirit.

Yurodivini - A Fool for Christ's sake.

SELECT BIBLIOGRAPHY

_____, *Early Fathers from the Philokalia*, tr. E. Kadloubovsky and G.E.H. Palmer (Boston, MA: Faber and Faber, 1954).

_____, *The Philokalia: The Complete Text*, 5 vols., tr. G.E.H. Palmer, Philip Sherrard, Kallistos Ware (Boston, MA: Faber and Faber, 1979-).

_____, *The Way of the Pilgrim and The Pilgrim Continues His Way*, tr. Helen Bacovcin (New York: Doubleday, 1978).

Arseniev, Nicholas, *Mysticism and the Eastern Church*, tr. Arthur Chambers (Crestwood, NY: Saint Vladimir's, 1979).

Russian Piety, tr. Asheleigh Moorehouse (Clayton, WI: American Orthodox Press, 1964).

Bolshakoff, Serge, *Russian Mystics*, Cistercian Studies Series 26 (Kalamazoo, MI: Cistercian Publications, 1977).

with M. Basil Pennington, o.c.s.o., *In Search of True Wisdom: Visits to Eastern Spiritual Fathers* (New York: Doubleday, 1979; New York: Alba House, 1991).

Brianchaninov, Ignatius, *On the Prayer of Jesus*, tr. Father Lazarus (London: John M Watkins, 1965).

Goldfrank, David, *The Monastic Rule of Josif Volotsky*, Cistercian Studies Series 83 (Kalamazoo, MI: Cistercian Publications, 1986).

Hausherr, Irenee, S.J., *Penthos. The Doctrine of Compunction in the Christian East*, Cistercian Studies Series 53 (Kalamazoo, MI: Cistercian Publications, 1982).

The Name of Jesus, tr. Charles Cummings, o.c.s.o., Cistercian Studies Series 44 (Kalamazoo, MI: Cistercian Publications, 1978).

Lossky, Vladimir, *The Mystical Theology of the Eastern Church* (London: James Clarke, 1957).

Maloney, George A., S.J., *Russian Hesychasm: The Spirituality of Nil Sorskij* (The Hague: Mouton, 1973).

Mother Maria, *The Jesus Prayer* (Filgrave: Greek Orthodox Monastery of the Assumption, 1972).

Meyendorff, John, *Byzantine Theology: Historical Trends and Doctrinal Themes* (New York: Fordham, 1974).

A Monk of the Eastern Church, *Orthodox Spirituality: An Outline of the Orthodox Ascetical and Mystical Tradition* (London: S.P.C.K., 1957).

Pennington, M. Basil, o.c.s.o., ed., *One Yet Two: Monastic Tradition East and West*, Cistercian Studies Series 29 (Kalamazoo, MI: Cistercian Publications, 1976).

O Holy Mountain: Journal of a Retreat on Mount Athos (New York: Doubleday, 1978; Wilmington, DE: Michael Glazier, 1988).

Ponticus, Evagrius, *Praktikos: Chapters on Prayer*, tr. John Eudes Bamberger, o.c.s.o., Cistercian Studies Series 4 (Spencer, MA: Cistercian Publications, 1970).

Sherrard, Philip, *Athos: The Holy Mountain* (Woodstock, NY: Overlook Press, 1982).

Spidlik, Tomas, S.J., *The Spirituality of the Christian East: A Systematic Handbook*, Cistercian Studies Series 79 (Kalamazoo, MI: Cistercian Publications, 1986).

Symeon, The New Theologian, *The Practical and Theological Chapter and the Three Theological Discourses*, tr. Paul McGuckin, C.P., Cistercian Studies Series 41 (Kalamazoo, MI: Cistercian Publications, 1982).